THE PRODIGAL WRITES FROM HIS HEART

ISBN 978-1-892230-27-0

By Bob Steinkamp

Rejoice Marriage Ministries, Inc.
Post Office Box 10548
Pompano Beach, FL 33061 USA

www.rejoiceministries.org

Scripture Quotations are from the King James Version or
the Holy Bible, New International Version. Copyright
1984, International Bible Society. Used by permission.

PRINTED IN THE UNITED STATES OF AMERICA

D0557231

Dedicated to our children and their families,

Tim, Patti, Allyson and Madison
Scott, Lori, Kayla, Kyle, Ryan and Ashley
Tom, Kathleen, Samantha and your unborn child

Bob's desire was for our children and grandchildren to not live through the generational curse of divorce in their lifetime and future generations.

TABLE OF CONTENTS

Holiday Devotionals

ACKNOWLEDGMENTS

How can anyone say "Thank You" to someone who picked up the baton and went running with it to the finish line? I am writing about our daughter, Lori who has been working for our ministry part-time for the past eleven years.

Every week we receive emails and letters saying how much Bob's Tuesday's Devotionals mean to them. One day I said to Lori, "I believe we are to compile many of Dad's devotionals in a book." Lori, who is so much like her father being so efficient and driven like her dad accepted the book project and compiled many of Bob's devotionals that are not in other books. Lori has since learned all the steps to starting and finishing a manuscript.

Kim Abegglen is no stranger to the process of getting a manuscript from our minds to the printer, as she has helped with many of our books. This one is no exception. Kim worked tirelessly to help see that others would be able to be blessed by the many devotionals that Bob has penned through the years.

Julie Bell, a Rejoice Marriage Ministries Board member has also worked on many books for us over the years. Julie again offered her expertise to help proof and edit Bob's manuscript this year. What a blessing to have Julie work with us on another one of Bob's books.

Amy Allen has become a friend of our family as we have grown close to her husband, Steve, an Associate Pastor and friend to our daughter, Lori and her husband, Scott. Amy is more than qualified to edit and proof our books and she is always willing to jump in and help complete the task.

Kathleen Steinkamp and Renee Bush spent hours checking scriptures to make sure that no mistakes slipped through the cracks.

A special thanks to Kirk at Kingdom, Inc. who took Lori's vision for the cover artwork and created a masterpiece.

May the Lord bless each of you for all your help; you were an answer to my prayers.

Charlyne Steinkamp

INTRODUCTION

In 1985, after years of playing church and a turbulent marriage, my dad, Bob Steinkamp, finally left home for the last time. My mom, Charlyne, thought that a divorce would be the fix to the years of abuse and unfaithfulness.

It wasn't long after their divorce that the Lord used a Christian singing group visiting our church to plant the seed of restoration in my mom's heart. This couple told of their troubles and how the Lord changed them and restored their marriage.

At this time, my dad was involved with another woman and he had no intention of coming back home. That day, my mom invited him to go with her to the evening service and hear this couple speak. Of course, he declined, thinking she must have lost her mind.

That day started a journey of restoration for my mom, first with the Lord, then with her husband. She began to see Bob how the Lord saw him, not as the wretched sinner he was. She also began to get herself in a right relationship with the Savior, knowing that until Christ was the center of her life, her relationships couldn't be pure.

As you can imagine, my dad was not thrilled to hear my mom was "standing" for their marriage to be restored. Frankly, my brothers and I were not either. In time, we saw the change the Lord was making in my mom's life and we knew something bigger was at work.

Two and a half years after their divorce, my dad came home suddenly. It was so sudden that he had to call the other woman that night and explain he would not be over for dinner because he remarried his wife earlier in the day.

That day a journey of healing began that was later birthed into Rejoice Marriage Ministries. Rejoice Marriage

Ministries exists to help others see that God does heal hurting marriages.

My dad always had a heart for the prodigals, because he was once right where they are. He knew the pulls that are felt toward sin and the pulls that are felt toward home.

Each week, we receive many emails that state what an encouragement the daily *Charlyne Cares* devotionals are to men and women who are standing for the healing of their broken marriage. Over the years, my dad has penned many devotionals. Many of these emails state that the Tuesday, *Prodigal's Perspective*, written by Bob, is just what they needed to hear that day.

After my dad's death in December 2010, it became apparent that the Lord was not done using my dad's words to minister to others. We received numerous requests to continue the *Prodigal's Perspective* devotionals. My mom felt the Lord was telling her that we should put together one more book of devotions written by a former prodigal.

From that conversation, *A Prodigal Writes From His Heart*, was birthed. I have had a wonderful time reading the hundreds of devotionals that my dad has written through the years as we chose a few for this book. My dad had a way of telling stories that draw you in, but he was also always transparent in regards to his former life in sin.

My prayer for you is that you will see through my dad's life that we do serve a God of miracles. We serve a God who wants to change each of us into His likeness for His glory.

As you will see through this book, after my parents' remarriage, it didn't mean the end of tests and trials for our family. The difference was that after their remarriage, we witnessed God's faithfulness in a way that only He could provide.

Jesus Christ loves you, and He loves your prodigal. I hope as you read through the pages of this book, you will sense His overwhelming love for your family.

God does heal hurting and dead marriages!

Lori Steinkamp Lassen

I HATE DIVORCE

*"You must obey my laws and be careful to follow my decrees. I am the LORD your God. Keep my decrees and laws, for the man who obeys them will live by them. I am the LORD." **Leviticus 18:4-5***

It would be impossible for anyone to read the letters and email that Charlyne and I do each day and not have something change in one's heart. The devastation and destruction that the enemy wants to bring to families is beyond explanation. Every time I feel like we have heard every possible means of satanic attack, we hear of a new means of attack that is almost beyond belief.

What has changed in my heart? I hate divorce more than ever. Before you get offended that my words are too strong, please allow me to share the Word of God:

*Has not the LORD made them one? In flesh and spirit they are his. And why one? Because he was seeking godly offspring. So guard yourself in your spirit, and do not break faith with the wife of your youth." "I hate divorce," says the LORD God of Israel, "and I hate a man's covering himself with violence as well as with his garment," says the LORD Almighty. So guard yourself in your spirit, and do not break faith. **Malachi 2:15-16***

If the God I serve hates divorce, I will also. I also hate everything associated with divorce. Why would society embrace and accept with an approving wink what God clearly tells us that He hates?

I hate seeing men and women abandoned because a prodigal mate, blinded by sin, wanted to exchange responsibility for fun.

I hate hearing how the people we work with cannot pay their bills because their spouse has abandoned them.

1

I hate having to explain to a little guy or girl that they are not the reason their Daddy or Mama left them.

I hate seeing kids having their childhood stolen by an absent, selfish prodigal parent.

I hate seeing standers, driving old cars without even enough money to eat properly, much less to have an ounce of fun in life.

I hate hearing about a stander who does not even have a place to call home because of divorce and what some court had ordered.

I hate reading how older women have to go into the workforce for the first time. Instead of enjoying their golden years, they are struggling to get and maintain a minimal job, just to survive.

I hate learning that a stander who has serious medical problems, probably because of the stress of divorce, cannot even afford proper medical treatment or medication.

I hate knowing that male standers are prohibited from spending time with their kids as God intended, because some judge, about to go home to his own family, signed a petition without considering what it would do to the people involved.

I hate knowing that female standers have to do things God never intended for them to do such as home repairs, just to keep their dwelling intact.

I hate hearing how much "fun" a prodigal spouse thinks they are having after dumping their family for some young thing. (Sin is fun for a season, but there is always a great price to pay afterward, both in this life and in the eternity beyond).

I hate hearing of bad advice from counselors, family, pastors, and friends to "Get on with your life," and that "God has someone better."

I hate the mockery the legal system makes out of the covenant of marriage.

I hate seeing how much our people hurt.

I hate how prodigals cry when showing us photos of their beloved spouse for life who has become a prodigal.

I love prodigals to the bone and pray that God will open their eyes and send them home from synthetic make-believe worlds, such as I once lived in. I woke up today hating divorce more today than I did yesterday. It is just not right! Will you stand with me in hating divorce?

Ten Reasons to Go Home

1. You promised God on your wedding day that you would keep your husband or wife forever. Leaving them is breaking your promise to God. We need to be covenant keepers and not covenant breakers.

2. Your children are being placed at a disadvantage that will follow them all of their lives. Studies have shown they will have increased risk of everything from lower grades, to risk of going to jail, to failure of their own marriages if they are not raised by both mother and father together.

3. Divorce is a poor example to your extended family and to your circle of friends.

4. Statistically, you will live longer at home with your family with the absence of stress over divorce.

5. Divorce drastically drops the economic standard of living for both men and women. In short, you will probably have much more money at home than living apart.

6. You, your spouse, and any children will see God work in bringing you home, so that each of you can understand that no problem in the future is too big for God.

7. True happiness can be found only at home living with the person you married.

8. After individuals fall, families fall. After families fall, churches fall. After churches fall, a society falls. By doing your part in the restoration of your family, you are being a responsible member of society.

9. After you learn that God has the power to heal marriages, you and your spouse can look to Him together for any crisis your family will ever face.

10. It is what God desires, demands and expects. We gave up prayer in school and we accepted abortion. Are we going to now give up the family and accept four, five, six, (or more) marriages as normal? God have mercy!

Here's the bottom line of your going home: Are you going to be obedient to God or are you going to continue to be disobedient? With obedience comes God's blessing. With continued disobedience, your life will never be near all that God intended it to be.

If you fully obey the LORD your God and carefully follow all his commands I give you today, the LORD your God will set you high above all the nations on earth. All these blessings will come upon you and accompany you if you obey the LORD your God: You will be blessed in the city and blessed in the country. **Deuteronomy 28:1-3**

CHOOSE TO BELIEVE

One Monday night at Bible study, my wife used the above phrase several times in her teaching. At one point, she said something poetic by accident, "You need to choose to believe. That's the only way you will be free." As often happens, she continued with part of her own testimony. It seemed almost as if she were giving each of the lines below in her teaching. The Lord started my wheels turning, and a few minutes later I shared these words with our group:

> *The thief came a - knocking at my front door,*
> *So I told my spouse there would be no more.*
> *"You have the 'escape clause,'" many told me,*
> *I expected after a divorce to be happy and free.*
>
> *Something's wrong, I thought, alone each night,*
> *But why do I hurt when divorce seemed so right?*
> *There is something amiss here when I hurt so,*
> *My spouse sinned, but my tears they do flow.*
>
> *Over and over the Lord God attempted to talk to me,*
> *All I could do was worry about my mate being free.*
> *Lord, I tried and failed doing it the world's way,*
> *What, dear God, to me can you promise, do and say?*
>
> *"Dear child, you can choose to believe My way today,*
> *Divorce is not the answer, no matter what others say.*
> *All the prodigal spouses around - no problem for Me,*
> *For them, My son, Jesus, bled and died upon the tree.*
> *Today take a stand for your marriage to be made new,*
> *With this being alone and hurting you can be through.*
> *The path is not easy; I will lead all along the way,*
> *After I, your God speaks to you, what can anyone say?"*
>
> *So now I am a stander, with Jesus as my best Friend,*
> *Yes, Lord, yes, I choose to believe You to the end.*

I believe that my spouse is on the way home tonight,
Enemy Satan, evil one, you just lost another fight!

Friend, Charlyne and I pray that you will choose to believe as you make the spiritual journey toward a healed home. May your stand be strong, not because you have heard from the Steinkamps, but because you have heard from the Lord.

So do not throw away your confidence; it will be richly rewarded. You need to persevere so that when you have done the will of God, you will receive what he has promised. **Hebrews 10:35-36**

I pray that today you will start the process, be it ever so slow, to develop a consistent life. That is what your prodigal wants. Remember, your beloved is not listening to how loud you shout about faith and change; the one you love is watching how straight you walk.

"I have set you an example that you should do as I have done for you. I tell you the truth, no servant is greater than his master, nor is a messenger greater than the one who sent him. Now that you know these things, you will be blessed if you do them." **John 13:15-17**

"GOD, CHANGE MY SPOUSE"

But whatever was to my profit I now consider loss for the sake of Christ. What is more, I consider everything a loss compared to the surpassing greatness of knowing Christ Jesus my Lord, for whose sake I have lost all things. I consider them rubbish, that I may gain Christ and be found in him, not having a righteousness of my own that comes from the law, but that which is through faith in Christ—the righteousness that comes from God and is by faith.
Philippians 3:7-9

Saturday morning I was reading overnight email when one grabbed my attention. The stander began her message, ***"Today God opened my eyes."*** Those five words suddenly had my undivided attention. What had happened to this wife was exactly the experience Charlyne and I pray for each and every man and woman seeking marriage restoration. One more person had been touched to do things God's way and not the world's way.

After reading that brief message, I moved on to a number of other emails, but each one was distinctly different from that first message. The difference that made that email stand out was exactly what brought me home over 25 years ago. Please let me explain.

I was brought home, not by the changes God made in my life, because they came after the fact. I started looking toward home, first out of criticism, then out of curiosity, and finally out of conviction, because of sincere, heartfelt changes that I witnessed and heard about from our kids. These changes were taking place in my wife's life and heart.

I know now, having read Charlyne's journals from those days that she was praying and fasting for changes in my life. But even greater, my wife was allowing God to change her in every area.

Please do not think I am diminishing the importance of prayer in any way, but what is going to most effectively grab the attention of a sinful prodigal spouse and touch their heart: learning their sins have been laid bare on 28 online prayer lists, or witnessing real changes taking place in the heart of their one-flesh spouse?

Most of our email, especially prayer requests, deals with the change the stander is asking God to make in the life of a prodigal spouse. It is rare to receive a message where a man or woman is asking God to change them. The number of messages we receive in which someone is praising God for opening their eyes is not as common.

Apart from the first reference asking for prayer, many of the prayer requests we receive mention neither God nor the work of the Holy Spirit. Even when their mate's faults are freely shared, any references to how the writer needs God to work in their own life are absent. What was the old saying about it taking two to tango?

What is the first step in marriage restoration? The stander must ask God to literally turn them inside out, revealing and exposing anything the Lord desires to change in every area of their being. Certainly, the stander prays and fasts for their prodigal spouse, but the focus, the main area of concern transfers from "them" to "me." Allow God to work in your life and give Him the responsibility for your prodigal spouse.

Nothing, absolutely nothing, will attract the attention of your prodigal spouse like the Holy Spirit being allowed to work in your life. The starting point for that to happen is forgiveness. Once you have started the day to day process of forgiving your spouse, there is not much to put in an email prayer request because there is not much fault left.

Charlyne had a hundred and one reasons to hate me, starting with adultery and abuse and continuing right down through the alphabet. Nevertheless, she chose to forgive me for all the past as well as the future. The day she called me asking me to forgive her for her part in our marriage failure, was only the start of changes I would observe in the woman I had married nineteen years prior.

For if you forgive men when they sin against you, your heavenly Father will also forgive you. But if you do not forgive men their sins, your Father will not forgive your sins. **Matthew 6:14-15**

Before you attempt to run a play from my wife's play book and fumble, be warned there is nothing we prodigals can spot faster than cries of forgiveness that are only skin deep or a relationship with Christ that is lived out in word, but not in deed. If you attempt to make minor adjustments to your life, intending that your prodigal will take them to be from the heart, the cause of your marriage restoration will be severely damaged.

Love must be sincere. Hate what is evil; cling to what is good. Be devoted to one another in brotherly love. Honor one another above yourselves. **Romans 12:9-10**

Why would anyone desire a superficial relationship with Christ or do less than forgiving from the heart and in all sincerity? Once you surrender your life to the Lord and He starts changing you, someone you love will do like I did with Charlyne and start to take notice.

Please allow God to change you first. Then He will change your prodigal spouse and one more marriage will be on the road to restoration. Granted, it may be slow going, with many detours along the way, but, thank God, you are on the right road.

Not that I have already obtained all this, or have already been made perfect, but I press on to take hold of that for which Christ Jesus took hold of me. Brothers, I do not

consider myself yet to have taken hold of it. But one thing I do: Forgetting what is behind and straining toward what is ahead, I press on toward the goal to win the prize for which God has called me heavenward in Christ Jesus.
Philippians 3:12-14

A QUICK START GUIDE TO STANDING

Who is wise? He will realize these things. Who is discerning? He will understand them. The ways of the LORD are right; the righteous walk in them, but the rebellious stumble in them. **Hosea 14:9**

If you have ever unpacked a new printer or some other computer accessory, underneath the Styrofoam packing, you probably discovered a thick operating manual. My first thought each time I open something new is that I will never master everything in the manual. Dig a bit deeper into the box and you will probably find a quick start guide, with just enough information to allow you to start using your new device. It is not intended to answer all the questions, but only to point you in the right direction.

I would like to give you a quick start guide for standing. Much like a new printer, this is not the total manual, but a few tips to both head you in the right direction and help you avoid mistakes. The complete Manual is found in the Holy Bible. To be a successful stander, you need to read and meditate on the Bible daily.

Based on what my wife and I have heard from people just like you for over 20 years, here is our quick start guide, which could also be called *"22 Facts About Standing:"*

My people are destroyed from lack of knowledge. . . **Hosea 4:6 (NKJV)**

1. Do not expect people to understand or support your stand for marriage restoration. God has given you, not others, the assignment and the burden to stand with Him and pray for your spouse. Because of this, you must always look to God and not to people for your support.

2. The day you promise God that you will stand for your marriage, you become like a lightning rod for attacks from the enemy. Expect to be tempted in ways you never imagined. Anticipate the circumstances to become worse. Know that you and your family are now a threat to the work of Satan. The evil one and his demons will attempt in every way to get you to give up. If you are a lightning rod for satanic attacks, Jesus Christ is your Ground. He alone can protect you from every harm.

If you forgive anyone, I also forgive him. And what I have forgiven—if there was anything to forgive—I have forgiven in the sight of Christ for your sake, in order that Satan might not outwit us. For we are not unaware of his schemes. **2 Corinthians 2:10-11**

3. Always remember that this is a spiritual battle, and spiritual battles are won with spiritual weapons. Following someone's secular program in hopes of marriage restoration is like going into war in Iraq armed only with a toy water pistol.

4. Your beloved mate has been taken captive by Satan to do his evil will. The words and actions that hurt you today are those of the enemy and not your spouse. Remember, Satan is the father of all lies, so do not expect to hear the truth from your prodigal spouse.

5. One way or another, your prodigal will witness or hear about your changed lifestyle when you start looking to God alone to heal and restore your marriage and family. Your prodigal, with their life in a tailspin, will be strangely attracted to the peace you have, in spite of the circumstances. Claim that peace by a consistent, close, loving relationship with Jesus Christ. The peace that attracts prodigals comes from God alone, not from any self-help or secular program designed to get your spouse back in the door.

6. Always remember, this is not about coaxing or manipulating your prodigal spouse back home so that you will be happy. It is a life or death battle for the eternal destiny of your prodigal's soul. The end result will be life eternal in Heaven or Hell, depending on what your beloved does with Jesus.

7. Your stand is about much more than you and your spouse. It is also about your family, your circle of influence, your future generations, and even people you may not even know who are silently following your example.

8. In most instances, your prodigal spouse is better off living in your home than outside. We understand there are safety and health factors that must be considered, but forcing them to leave the family home is often turning them out to Satan's playground. As long as they are in the home, you can better detect your mate's spiritual needs and thus pray for them.

9. Expect every area of your mate's life to change as they silently seek relief from the torment the enemy is bringing their way. Do not be wiped out by job changes, moves to distant places, new hobbies and attractions, or even an often-forced attempt to legalize their adultery by entering into a non-covenant marriage to another person. If you are standing strong, God still considers you to be married.

10. Regardless of why your spouse left home, and in spite of what they are saying, most prodigals become involved with another person during their far country experience. Do not be devastated if that happens.

11. No matter what professional-sounding tag has been attached to your wayward spouse, the bottom line is that every husband or wife who has ever walked out on a marriage has done so because of sin. Your beloved might have a sex, substance or selfishness problem. They might have been diagnosed, often by a professional who has never met them, with a chemical imbalance, bi-polar disorder, or mid-life issues. Regardless, they still have a sin problem. Marriages are healed when spouses stop making excuses with man's terms and start dealing with their mate's sin problem in the prayer closet.

12. No other human can tell you the exact day your prodigal will repent and come home. We know of too many good standers who have been almost destroyed when someone traveling through town prophesies an exact date for restoration, and that date comes and goes without anything happening. The date is God's business and not man's. As a stander, you need to live every day as though today was your day of restoration. Wake up every day looking down the front walk and ask God if this is the day.

13. Allow God to be God in bringing your prodigal home to Himself and home to you. Be careful not to set stipulations for your prodigal's return without first seeking God for His will.

14. Standing is not reciting a prayer, nor is it attending meetings, or talking the talk of a stander. It must become a way of life for you. That way of life is living like Jesus did. There must be no place for sin in any form in your life. If you call yourself a stander, you must want to see how far from the line called sin you can live. Do not experiment with what God will allow you to get away with. The sinful things of this world must be constantly dropping from your life, as they are replaced by the things of God. For example, developing a desire for Christian music that will help you praise the Lord, it will quiet your heart, it will help you support your stand instead of music from the world. Live a holy life.

15. Standing is not learned, nor is it mastered all at once. It is learned one step (or one mistake) at a time. God allows for mistakes in standing as you learn. I cannot tell you how many times each month a person who is serious about standing tells us how they have "really blown it" with their

Lord God or with their mate. God allows mistakes, and He forgives them when we repent. The only way you can "really blow it" is by giving up on God and on your prodigal spouse. Even then, God allows fresh starts. Somehow, He covers over all your mistakes, when you sincerely repent, like the tide washing across the beach. Every sign of imperfection is washed away.

16. If standing becomes "too hard" and you "can't do it anymore," and you give up standing, nothing is going to be any different about your life tomorrow. Your prodigal spouse will be the same, as will your circumstances. The only difference is that you have given up your hope and, in effect have bought into, "the idea that some things are impossible even for God." This simply is not true. If you limit God in marriage restoration, you are also limiting Him every time you need Him in the future. Nothing is impossible with God.

17. Another hard fact of standing is that you should stay away from and not accept advice from people named "They." We often hear how "They feel God has someone better for me," or "They said I should get on with my life." When "They" say your my marriage is hopeless, we want to reply, "It's not about what "They" say, but about what God says. You cannot be listening to "They" and God at the same time."

The heart of the discerning acquires knowledge; the ears of the wise seek it out. **Proverbs 18:15**

18. You might have heard me say previously that if there had been an Internet and email 20 years ago when we were divorced and Charlyne was standing with God and praying for me, I am not certain that I would be here today. If I, as a prodigal spouse, had read some of the things about me that even good standers post all over the Internet today, I would have run the opposite direction. It is almost as if today's standers think they are having a private conversation with a friend, when they diagnose and disclose the mate's faults and weaknesses online. There is Internet access in the pigpens of life also. Prodigals read the message boards and chat rooms–and additional damage is done to already troubled marriages.

19. It is a fact that God is on your side. His Word has direction for every situation you will ever face. People may declare, based on human reasoning, "It's over," but God never does.

20. Do not allow other hurting people to help "fix" your problems. If they can't "fix" their own problems, why allow them to have input in to yours? That is God's job, not one for other humans.

21. The prodigal journey home is filled with false starts. Please be prepared for these. Standers are being wiped out by, "He/She came home yesterday and left again today." This is all part of the prodigal process. You must be aware of and praying against the spiritual battle that is raging for your beloved. (As an aside, let me say that most prodigals who are on the way home are doing the very best they can, in light of their absence of spiritual weapons for this spiritual battle. That is why your prayers are so important.)

22. Prodigals do come home. We come home, not to people who are dabbling in standing. We come home to spouses who are serious about their relationship with Jesus Christ and serious about praying their spouse away from Hell. We come home to standers who are not blown away by the unexpected. We come home to praying spouses who have not set deadlines for God, nor for us. We come home to standing and waiting spouses who strive to cover our sinful nakedness in front of others, not share everything they know or suspect. We prodigals come home to spouses who are walking with God 100% of the way. May you start today to be the kind of godly stander that prodigals come home to (often suddenly!).

And this is my prayer: that your love may abound more and more in knowledge and depth of insight, so that you may be able to discern what is best and may be pure and blameless until the day of Christ, filled with the fruit of righteousness that comes through Jesus Christ—to the glory and praise of God. **Philippians 1:9-11**

"HOW DID WE GET TO THIS POINT?"

"We all, like sheep, have gone astray, each of us has turned to his own way; and the LORD has laid on him the iniquity of us all." **Isaiah 53:6**

Even though the ministry office is only half a mile away, each time one of our children married and moved away from home, their former bedroom was drafted into ministry service. As a result, Charlyne and I often work at home in two offices that are in opposite ends of our house.

One evening after dinner, we each had work and agreed to meet back in the family room at 9:00 P.M. We had spent our evening reading and hearing about prodigal spouses.

Do you know the primary question that many of these prodigals are asking themselves? "How did we get to this point?" No man or woman suddenly wakes up and states, "Good morning. This might be a great day to dump my family, along with my faith." No, Satan is far more subtle than that. The evil one planted a seed of temptation, watered it with opportunity, and fertilized it with selfishness. That thing continued to grow until it took over a family, and causes someone to ask, "How did we get to this point?"

After our quitting time that evening, we turned the television on. A news report was being given on a fourteen-year-old from foster care who had been shot and killed late at night while driving a stolen car. The report was followed by an ad for a new television program that depicted virginity as a joke. The ad was nothing short of vulgar. The second ad that followed was for engine oil, but a locker room phrase had been carefully woven into it. That was more than I could take, so I paused the television and turned to Charlyne to ask, "How did we get to this point?"

What has happened to society, including the church that we joke about what is sacred and gloss over family tragedy? "How did we get to this point?"

I awoke several times that night, thinking about that question. How did society get to the point that we can't even decide what is right and what is wrong? How did we get to the point that men of God are suggesting divorce to hurting couples? How did we get to the point that serial marriages are acceptable, that is being married to several people one at a time? How did we get to the point that the child abuse called divorce is being inflicted on children by the courts?

Giving thought to the question, I discovered the answer to how we got to this point. It was because of me. As a former prodigal husband, I need to accept responsibility for things being in the shape they are in today.

When I walked out on my family, I damaged far more than just our family. One link in a local church was taken out by our divorce. That weakened church also weakens society. Sadly, things are like they are today because of me and others like me. Television networks can make a mockery of virginity, marriage, Christmas, Christians and so much more because of what we, as an individual, allowed, by example, to be set into place.

When a prodigal spouse asks their mate, "How did we get to this point?" they already know the answer. They are really asking, "How do we get back to where we should be?"

Once individuals become what they should be, with Jesus Christ central, our families can become what they should be. When our families are all they should be, can't you see how our churches will be strengthened? Strong churches have always been the basis of a strong society.

But now that you have been set free from sin and have become slaves to God, the benefit you reap leads to holiness, and the result is eternal life. For the wages of sin is death, but the gift of God is eternal life in Christ Jesus our Lord. **Romans 6:22-23**

"How do we get back to where we should be?" It matters not if it is an individual, a family, a church or a society posing the question. The answer remains the same: ***by turning back to the Lord God, our Creator.*** If we continue on the slide of self-destruction, family destruction and church destruction, we will witness society's destruction. Someone needs to put on the brakes. That someone is me and you.

What is the starting point of restoration of families, churches, and society? Each of us must turn to our Lord God and allow Him to make us personally to be all He wants us to be. Once we learn how to listen and to follow Him in every way the dominos we have knocked down will start to stand up in succession once again.

May I ask you a hard question? Where are you today? Are you sold out to Jesus Christ, ready to serve Him and follow Him at any cost, or are you just along for the ride? Too often our "This is too hard so I quit" mail comes from people who are mis-using the term "stander" and possibly even the name "Christian." A real stander is never a quitter, because they realize the eternal destiny (Heaven or Hell) of a prodigal spouse could be at stake.

May you make this a time to get serious about standing so your prodigal will discover the answer to their "How do we get back to where we should be?" question by looking at you.

On the evening of July 7, 1987, as I sat on the edge of our bed, having just remarried Charlyne a few hours before, I asked myself, "How did we get to this point?" My answer over two decades ago was about the same as my answer today. We got there because I had a praying wife, serious about standing and willing to follow Jesus at any cost, until He healed our marriage.

There is a lot at stake. May you and I follow Jesus as He rebuilds people, families, churches and society according to His Master Plan.

"Follow my example, as I follow the example of Christ." **1 Corinthians 11:1**

DEEP REGRETS

Remember, O LORD, your great mercy and love, for they are from of old. Remember not the sins of my youth and my rebellious ways; according to your love remember me, for you are good, O LORD. **Psalm 25:6-7**

I have many regrets for what my selfish pursuits of pleasure did to our family. If God allows your prodigal spouse to stay on this earth long enough, they will also have regrets for what they have done to your family.

Regret, to me, is totally separate from forgiveness. God has forgiven me for what I did to my family. I sought Charlyne's forgiveness on the day we remarried in 1987, and many times since. Without a doubt, both my Lord and my wife have totally forgiven me. Nevertheless I have regrets over having become a prodigal.

The dictionary defines "regret" as "the emotion arising from a wish that some matter or situation could be different than what it is." I regret having been an abusive and unfaithful husband. My attention to the wrong things robbed three kids out of the guidance and direction that I should have been providing.

South Florida has been spared from Hurricane Ike, but somewhere, in a few days, some other unfortunate community will experience the eye of the storm. Do you know what the eye of a hurricane is like? It is total peace. No wind and no rain, because everything is swirling around that point.

A prodigal spouse, who reports experiencing such peace and serenity in their life today, is really living in the eye of the storm. They reached that point after weathering the storms of marriage trouble. They can be forgiven, by both spouse and God, but the only way out is by weathering the other side of the marriage storm: a storm of guilt and regret.

22

If they would only turn to the Lord, He would stop the howling winds of guilt.

The storms of regret may linger, even after total forgiveness is in place. Your prodigal may come home as the parent of a non-covenant child, or having created legal or financial problems while gone.

Please understand I have no regrets at remarrying Charlyne. All those things I did in the far country, the ones where I have said a thousand times, "I don't know how I could have done that stuff," are still accompanied by deep regret.

Recently, the family life of a godly vice presidential candidate has been literally taken apart by the media. The candidate has expressed they are a normal family with normal problems. Nevertheless, as some of their family issues are exposed to the world, both that husband and wife must be thinking, "If only we had. . ."

Let's go back to the Steinkamps on Seventh Street. Our marriage is good. The sex that I once went seeking elsewhere is now woo-hoo right here at home, but without the guilt. My wife and I enjoy ministering together and can almost finish each other's sentences. We are close to all three of our adult children and their spouses. None of our seven young grandchildren can enter our home without asking, "Where's Grandpa?"

Nevertheless, I have many regrets over what I did back then that are being played out today in our extended family. Much like the candidate's family, and like any family, we have issues. Foremost are the health concerns of our grandchildren. There are also employment and housing and health and financial concerns, not for us as much as for the people we love. Many times when a new challenge arises, I think, "If only I had. . ." The honest truth is that if I had been around, being the husband and daddy that I should have been, some of those situations would be playing out differently today.

Why am I sharing our family secrets today? To help you better understand your prodigal spouse. I want you to know the eye of the storm that your loved one seems to be happy and prosperous in today is deceptive. Charlyne and I also want you to know that your compassion and understanding can be the salve and bandage for your mate's painful wounds of regret.

Yes, we prodigals do come home with regrets. These pale when compared to the eternal regrets of having rejected God's call on us to leave a life of sin.

Do you not know that the wicked will not inherit the kingdom of God? Do not be deceived: Neither the sexually immoral nor idolaters nor adulterers nor male prostitutes nor homosexual offenders nor thieves nor the greedy nor drunkards nor slanderers nor swindlers will inherit the kingdom of God. And that is what some of you were. But you were washed, you were sanctified, you were justified in the name of the Lord Jesus Christ and by the Spirit of our God. **1 Corinthians 6:9-11**

A SITUATION LIKE MINE

So, if you think you are standing firm, be careful that you don't fall! No temptation has seized you except what is common to man. And God is faithful; he will not let you be tempted beyond what you can bear. But when you are tempted, he will also provide a way out so that you can stand up under it. ***1 Corinthians 10:12-14***

Every day we read letters and email from wounded and abandoned spouses. Many of these messages include the phrase, "You've probably never heard of *a situation like mine*." The writer then shares insight into what they feel made their marriage crumble.

Some of the *"situations like mine"* are indeed horrible. The crushed spouse may tell about their mate's former call by God to ministry. Some report a homosexual relationship or an affair with a best friend or a member of the extended family. We may read of sexual affairs born out of the best of intentions or even affairs with a person in ministry or with a counselor. Most people have concurrent problems, such as children problems, health problems, or devastating financial circumstances along with their marriage crisis.

After twenty years of ministering to hurting spouses, we can declare that Satan has no new tricks. Why should the evil one need to do anything different when families are still falling victim to the same schemes? Satan's desire is to convince you that your situation is so far from what other people experience that it is hopeless. The hopes of many people for marriage restoration have been destroyed when they listen to the enemy telling them their situation is peculiar to them alone.

Let's look at Noah. He was a man who had a situation like no other person had ever experienced. He didn't give up because of *"a situation like mine."* What is the difference between Noah and a stander looking at what they feel are

25

peculiar situations and giving up what God has called them to do? The outcome is determined by where you look and what you hear. Think about all that Noah must have heard from the enemy.

There's something else we need to consider about Noah. The Bible does not tell us that Noah fretted over how deep the flood water would become. He totally depended on God, regardless of what people said.

Remember Joseph, whose brothers sold him into slavery. He had every right to share about *"a situation like mine."* Look at Job. Now there was an individual who was in a unique situation, with Satan taking everything precious to Job. People, from Job's friends to his wife, attempted to convince Job that God had failed him. What happened to Job in the end? His God restored double to Job everything he had lost, all because Job remained faithful during his adversity.

We do not want in any way to discredit what you are experiencing today. We do want to remind you that we serve a Lord God who can handle a situation like yours, when you surrender your will and your way to Him. Will you?

Do not conform any longer to the pattern of this world, but be transformed by the renewing of your mind. Then you will be able to test and approve what God's will is—his good, pleasing and perfect will. **Romans 12:2**

OVERLOOKING THE OBVIOUS

The LORD will guide you always; he will satisfy your needs in a sun-scorched land and will strengthen your frame. You will be like a well-watered garden, like a spring whose waters never fail. **Isaiah 58:11**

My printer had stopped working. I decoded the series of blinking lights on it to determine that it wanted a new drum. For reasons that I don't understand, a new printer was less expensive to purchase than it was going to be to buy the one component for the old machine.

If you are like me, we develop an attachment to our printers and are hesitant to change. As often happens, the old printer is no longer manufactured and a change in type of printer must be made. I knew how much paper to load and which programs it had trouble printing from. Best of all, I could almost change ink cartridges on the old printer in the dark, after having done it so many times.

My new printer arrived, and I said good-bye to the old one. The ever-present dust that had accumulated under the old machine was cleared away and the printer installed. Soon, that anticipated first document came rolling out of the printer. The test paper looked fine, but this simply did not seem like my printer. It looked different. It even sounded different.

I had discovered a long time ago that new printers come with a much smaller ink cartridge. I was ready for that, with a new cartridge, naturally of a new type, waiting to be installed. In a couple of weeks, the colored lights began to flash, but I was not ready to tackle learning to change the cartridge in a new printer. That happened at 2:35 A.M. on a Friday morning.

I often wake up sometime during the night and check the overnight email. Friday morning I discovered an email of a stander's emergency that I knew Charlyne would want to read and to pray about when the sun came up Friday. When I attempted to print that one page, the printer just <u>sat there and blinked its lights at me without printing.</u>

I was ready for the challenge and dove into changing the ink cartridge. The directions were followed and finally the printer door closed. I attempted to print the email again, and the printer blinked a strange code at me. I retraced my steps, assuming something did not seat right. Still, the lights only blinked yellow-red-yellow at me. The old cartridge was even re-inserted in hopes of coaxing one more page out of it. Yellow-red-yellow blinked again. I gave up and went back to bed, thinking how my old printer would never have done this to me.

After daylight on Friday, I tackled the printer problem again. After a few more attempts and just before re-packing the new cartridge to be returned as defective, I almost took the new printer apart. That is when I discovered that it was out of paper! I added a stack of paper and my many attempts to print that middle-of-the-night email came rolling out of the machine. Caught up in my printer problem, I had been overlooking the obvious.

Before you laugh too much at my stupidity in overlooking the obvious, consider your own circumstances. Your marriage has stopped being productive. From all the blinking lights, the tendency is for you to diagnose the problem. The indicator of adultery flashes intermittently with the light of substance abuse. Many people decode what they are seeing as mid-life crisis, bi-polar disorder, or some other clinical title.

Regardless of the name given to the problems, everyone around you is telling you that, like my printer, you would be better off to get a replacement than to attempt to repair the old marriage. Thankfully, God places a much higher value on refurbishing marriages than we do on refurbishing printers.

If Charlyne or I were to talk with you, without a doubt you would tell us about all the flashing lights in your marriage. People tend to get stalled on the major symptom of a marriage falling apart: that other person their spouse is involved with. We might hear about "the triple A lights" of alcoholism, abuse, adultery. You might even say, "My situation is different," but in truth the bottom line is that your situation is exactly like every other hurting marriage across the land. Your spouse has a sin problem.

The acts of the sinful nature are obvious: sexual immorality, impurity and debauchery; idolatry and witchcraft; hatred, discord, jealousy, fits of rage, selfish ambition, dissensions, factions and envy; drunkenness, orgies, and the like. I warn you, as I did before, that those who live like this will not inherit the kingdom of God. **Galatians 5:19-21**

If you were to pull out the Bible, our instruction manual for life, you could learn from this one passage that everything from sexual immorality to selfish ambitions are, ". . .acts of the sinful nature." God will tell you why those warning lights are flashing in your marriage.

It should come as a tremendous release to many standers that they do not need to fret over the circumstances. These things are to be expected from your spouse, because of their "sinful nature." I have to wonder what God could do if every stander we know, and there are many thousands, would stop focusing on the circumstances; stop attempting to diagnose their mate's problem by man-made terms, and simply pray against the sinful nature in the one they love. Would we not see marriages changed?

When my new printer arrived, it came with a label warning about its use stuck on top of the box and packing. If life were a printer, it might come packaged in a box with *Galatians 5:21* printed on top. Before it was put into use, we would see:

I warn you, as I did before, that those who live like this will not inherit the kingdom of God.

Your reason for standing can be found in that same verse. You are standing not to see your marriage restored. That will only be the by-product of your spouse no longer being controlled by the sinful nature. We are each cautioned in that verse that if your spouse dies in their sin, "those who live like this will not inherit the kingdom of God."

My new printer came with a brief quick start guide, (which I did not consult at 2:35 A.M. to see why the colored lights were flashing). I pray that **Galatians 5:19-21** will become your quick start guide for a healed and restored marriage, encouraging you to never give up on the spouse that you and our Lord God both love so very much.

"I was enraged by his sinful greed; I punished him, and hid my face in anger, yet he kept on in his willful ways. I have seen his ways, but I will heal him; I will guide him and restore comfort to him, creating praise on the lips of the mourners in Israel. Peace, peace, to those far and near," says the LORD. *"And I will heal them."* **Isaiah 57:17-19**

WHY DIDN'T YOU MARRY THE OTHER WOMAN?

Let them know that it is your hand, that you, O LORD, have done it. **Psalm 109:27**

I pray the Lord will help me as I take you the long way to get there, but the bottom line is that I did not marry the other woman because deep inside I knew that would be wrong. Charlyne and I were divorced, and the world and the law were saying to go on, but something was reminding me that I was still married.

I acknowledge that no two situations are the same. What your absent spouse is feeling might be totally different, but it does not take a NASA scientist to know there was something wrong. When I was in another man's home, attempting to make his kids happy, sitting at his table, eating food bought with his child support money, watching the television that his labor purchased, being the joy of his forsaken wife's life-and more. Meanwhile, my heartbroken wife and our three children were literally struggling to survive while they prayed that a husband and Dad would come to his senses and come back home where he belonged.

Sadly, most married people who walk out on a spouse have or will become involved with someone else. The natural progression of continued dating is toward marriage. Even though your absent spouse may desire that illicit arrangement to continue status quo, I can assure you that third person in your marriage is pushing and pushing toward marriage.

Those other people put prodigals under enormous pressure to get married. A praying spouse who is standing with God is a threat to a sinful relationship. These other people feel they can gain control if they are able to pressure the other person into marrying them. There is one big problem. God does not recognize these adulterous relationships as marriages, and He continues to convict the prodigal of his or her sinful ways, regardless of what the records down at the courthouse record.

Prodigals are handed ultimatums by that other person. We can walk out on a covenant husband or wife without even looking back, but tremble when the counterfeit hands down an "or else" dictate. From personal experience, the church that the other person and I were attending, (yes, prodigals attend church and listen to preachers declare Truth to other people), had a new sanctuary under construction. It was to be finished by Easter that year. I was told that we would be married before that date or our relationship would end.

I was also ordered to "get over" Charlyne before that time. How could a person I had known for only months be dictating that I "get over" a wife of nineteen years?

Much of what I went through will not be disclosed, but I feel led to share one incident that will always be remembered. The other person and I were finishing dinner at an Italian restaurant when I was paged by my employer. Back then, cell phones were still tethered inside automobiles, so I left my credit card on the table and went searching for a pay phone. When I returned, my dinner companion handed me the credit card and a receipt. "I just wanted to see how it will look," she explained.

I opened the receipt to see "Mrs. Robert E. Steinkamp" signed on it. I had never before seen that written in anyone's handwriting except Charlyne's. It just did not look right. I felt trapped. My indigestion that night did not come from Italian food, but from the thought there might soon be a "Mrs. Robert E. Steinkamp" who was not really "Mrs. Robert E. Steinkamp."

Sometime later, I heard a quote on the car radio that touched me deeply and has become one of my favorites. Martyred missionary Jim Elliot is quoted as having said, "*A man is no fool who gives up what he cannot keep to gain what he cannot lose."* The Holy Spirit revealed to me that I was giving up Charlyne, whom I could not lose, for someone else, a counterfeit wife, whom I could not keep.

Can you see what the Holy Spirit of God was doing, in response to Charlyne's prayers? He was sending arrow after arrow of His Truth to me and continued to do so until the bubble of selfishness that surrounded me was destroyed. That is when this prodigal came home.

As a stander, please do not feel that your prayers have been unsuccessful or that you have failed in marriage restoration if your spouse enters a non-covenant relationship. You have failed only if you give up. It is our Lord God's reputation that is on the line, not yours, and He will do exactly what He promised you, but in His timing and not in man's.

Here are my Five P's to help you when you are faced with your mate's non-covenant marriage:

Pray - Learn how to pray for your spouse who is being pressured into marriage.

Proposal - Remember, that other person most likely proposed marriage, not your mate.

Peace - Get the peace of God that He has your mate in His hand today, regardless of what words may have been mumbled to someone else. God is saying that you and your beloved are still married.

Purpose - Refocus your purpose in standing. Is it to get even with the other person and bring your mate home, or is it that all involved will come to a personal relationship with Jesus Christ?

Promise - Reclaim the promises that God has given you and hold fast to them. God never changes.

My comfort in my suffering is this: Your promise preserves my life. **Psalm 119:50**

A STANDER'S MAKEOVER

Brothers, I do not consider myself yet to have taken hold of it. But one thing I do: Forgetting what is behind and straining toward what is ahead, I press on toward the goal to win the prize for which God has called me heavenward in Christ Jesus. All of us who are mature should take such a view of things. And if on some point you think differently, that too God will make clear to you. Only let us live up to what we have already attained. **Philippians 3:13-16**

Charlyne and I only see Paige, the author of a guest Monday devotional, on the first Monday evening of each month, when she travels 170 miles round trip with her stander's group to attend Rejoice Pompano. One Monday night, we both noticed such a difference in this woman that I called her and her Bible study leader aside to compliment Paige on the change in the months that she has been standing. She gave the Lord full credit for the difference. None of her circumstances have changed. In fact, she faced court during the upcoming week. Nevertheless, God had done a total makeover on one more stander, from the heart out, giving her the glow of the Lord.

For as I have often told you before and now say again even with tears, many live as enemies of the cross of Christ. Their destiny is destruction, their god is their stomach, and their glory is in their shame. Their mind is on earthly things. But our citizenship is in heaven. And we eagerly await a Savior from there, the Lord Jesus Christ, who, by the power that enables him to bring everything under his control, will transform our lowly bodies so that they will be like his glorious body. **Philippians 3:18-21**

The change that Charlyne and I noticed in the writer of that devotional is exactly what we desire for you. Are you ready to get started on your own stander's makeover? Your Lord God is ready to do His work on you and on your life.

. . . You became very beautiful and rose to be a queen. And your fame spread among the nations on account of your beauty, because the splendor I had given you made your beauty perfect, declares the Sovereign LORD. **Ezekiel 16:13b, 14**

There are two parts to a stander's makeover. The larger part is done by God, and the second part is your work, so that you can be all that He intends you to be. God's part is the heart surgery, where your heart of stone becomes a heart of flesh.

Have you ever noticed the face of an individual who is mad and revengeful? Forget about the steam blowing out of their ears, their face still shows those emotions. Charlyne and I often meet standers who are so angry with their spouse that their jaw is taut and their teeth clenched when they tell their story. The expression of a contented person escapes them. Even fear of the future, when Christ is not being trusted, can often be seen on a person's face. The posture of some standers is rigid from all the negative emotions.

Consider how much an individual's appearance can change when they allow all of those negative emotions to be replaced by the peace that passes all understanding. That kind of peace comes only from a personal relationship with Jesus Christ, relinquishing every one of your problems to Him, and then trusting Him alone for your every need.

A stander's makeover does not start with cosmetics and clothes, but with changes on the inside done by the Lord, when we trust Him. Those changes, though, always work themselves out to the surface. Somehow, once standers start to feel better inside, most then desire to look better on the outside. You cannot, however, make changes on the outside when the inside is still raging. As the country preacher once said, "You can put lipstick on a pig, but it's still a pig."

Ladies, when you leave home to run an errand, what do you look like? Have you combed your hair and put on something besides the old tee-shirt that you wear every evening? What might happen if you ran into your spouse, or one of his family members? When you speak, they will notice the internal change, but it would be perfect if you gave them something to catch the eye also.

Men, we are no different. Why shave when it's the weekend? Because this might be the day your wife sees you. The old shorts are comfortable, and go well with your uncombed hair, but what are you going to do when you meet your wife, head-on in the grocery store?

Before long, guess who has either witnessed the changes, or else is being told about them by family and friends? We prodigals! It happened to my wife, and God brought me home.

As an old hymn instructs:

"His power can make you what you ought to be;

His blood can cleanse your heart and make you free;

His love can fill your soul, and you will see,

Twas best for Him to have His way with thee."

(Song – *"His Way With Thee"* - Public Domain)

"The Spirit of the LORD will come upon you in power, and you will prophesy with them; and you will be changed into a different person. Once these signs are fulfilled, do whatever your hand finds to do, for God is with you."
I Samuel 10:6-7

Two words of caution need to be given regarding standers' makeovers. Modesty and dignity must be key to your clothes, your actions, and where you go. Do not wear, do, say, or go anywhere that you would ever be ashamed of your spouse hearing about, because they probably will.

Secondly, be on guard against unwanted and inappropriate attention from the opposite sex, as you and the Lord make your changes. Always remember that you are a married man or woman, regardless of what flattery might come your way. If someone is suddenly attracted to you, they are being attracted to the Jesus that is shining from within you.

Did you notice how I handled talking with Paige? I felt led to comment on her changes, which I knew had originated in the heart. Instead of talking to her alone, I invited her Bible study teacher into that conversation and, before giving the compliment, clarified why the third person was standing there. Both ladies knew clearly, before I gave the compliment, where I was coming from.

Yes, we prodigals do come home, in God's perfect time. A prodigal's free will is often touched when he or she encounters their spouse who has had a stander's makeover. Let's get started today on allowing God to make you what He desires for you to be, for Him and for your spouse.

To him who is able to keep you from falling and to present you before his glorious presence without fault and with great joy—to the only God our Savior be glory, majesty, power and authority, through Jesus Christ our Lord, before all ages, now and forevermore! Amen. **Jude 1:24**

REMINDERS

So I will always remind you of these things, even though you know them and are firmly established in the truth you now have. **2 Peter 1:12**

Somewhere along the way I became something of an amateur rock collector. Sitting atop the bookcase in my office are several large rocks that I have picked up on ministry travel. There is one large boulder from under the bridge that is pictured on the front of *Pulpits in the Marketplace*. Another was picked up outside of a church in Chattanooga. Many of these are simply limestone. They have no value or meaning to anyone other than me, but they do bring back memories to the Steinkamps.

On a one-day train trip to central Florida, I acquired something else to add to my collection. It is an old railroad spike, found near the Amtrak station in Sebring, Florida.

You may know that trains fascinate me. Thousands of tons of steel that have been formed into a train somehow ride atop two steel rails. If it were not for the spikes that secure the rails to the wooden cross ties, there would be no railroad as we know it today.

The spike that I recovered had obviously been used. The sharpened tip shows evidence of once having been driven into something. There are indentations on the head of the spike from having been hammered into place.

My new collection item has significance to me for another reason. Holding that rusty object in my hands, I realized once again the price that Jesus Christ paid for my sins and for yours. The spikes that held Jesus to that cross might have been like the one sitting beside me.

I sense that at times many of us are guilty of sanitizing the crucifixion until the real meaning of Jesus dying for us personally is lost in historical fact. My spike brings to me just a bit of the impact of the crucifixion. My first impression was to sand off the rust and paint the spike. On second thought, I have left the spike that sits atop my bookcase just as it is. May it always remind me that Jesus died for me.

Your marriage, in God's eyes, need not end with the banging of a judge's gavel. Your marriage is alive today because of sounds of spikes being driven into our Jesus on Calvary. May you and I never be guilty of trampling the cross by the careless handling of our marriage covenant.

Then he said to Thomas, "Put your finger here; see my hands. Reach out your hand and put it into my side. Stop doubting and believe". . .Then Jesus told him, "Because you have seen me, you have believed; blessed are those who have not seen and yet have believed." **John 20:27, 29**

SITUATIONAL STANDERS

"Haven't you read" he replied, "that at the beginning the Creator 'made them male and female,' and said, 'For this reason a man will leave his father and mother and be united to his wife, and the two will become one flesh'? So they are no longer two, but one. Therefore what God has joined together, let man not separate." **Matthew 19:4-6**

May I ask you a question? Regardless of your legal marital status, do you consider yourself to be married in God's eyes? I pray that you do, because that covenant between you, your spouse, and God is the very basis of your stand, praying and trusting God alone to heal and restore your marriage. It would take a miracle, you say? Yes, it would, but our God is a miracle working God.

There's a second question that needs to be asked. If you consider yourself married, are you acting like you are married 100% of the time? The physical absence or presence of your spouse has no bearing on your being married in God's eyes.

From what Charlyne and I are reading and hearing, far too many people to whom God has spoken His promise regarding the positive future of their marriage are becoming situational standers. Around other standers and marriage ministries, they talk the talk of a stander, but they then walk the walk of a single person. They are, in effect, like Sunday Christians, who attend church, Bible in hand, sing the songs, and go through the motions, but then for the rest of the week live not much different than the world does.

"Who will know if I am standing and acting single?" Foremost, you and God will know. In addition, your absent spouse just may know. A major television network followed a woman from the time she left her apartment until she arrived at work, and discovered how many security cameras captured her on the way. The number was amazing. Do you not feel that if multitudes of strangers can photograph us without our knowledge, that some of what you are doing, be it positive or negative, can filter back to your prodigal spouse?

Each Tuesday, on our *Charlyne Cares* devotionals we share the prodigal's perspective with you. I can say that I came home to a wife whose walk matched her talk 100% of the time. Charlyne was certainly not speaking the lingo of one standing with God and then acting differently.

You need to remember that Satan will turn every situation to his benefit, so you cannot afford to risk having your prodigal witness or hear of your single-type living. The future of your restored marriage may very well depend on your actions in these days.

Be self-controlled and alert. Your enemy the devil prowls around like a roaring lion looking for someone to devour. Resist him, standing firm in the faith. **I Peter 5:8-9a**

One Saturday morning while we were divorced, I called our home to arrange to pick up the children. Another man answered Charlyne's phone. He obviously knew of me, but refused to say who he was, or why he was in our family home. He refused to call Charlyne to the phone. I suspected that my wife had "gone on with her life" and I was devastated. It turned out that two church families had discovered all that Charlyne needed doing around the home, and had shown up on that Saturday for a work day. Charlyne and the ladies had gone to the store, and the man was being helpful in answering the ringing phone for my absent wife.

I pray that you can realize how the enemy is out to turn the best of intentions into a mess, into something that will do additional damage to your family. You must do everything possible to avoid that happening. To do so you must always live, act, behave, and talk as married.

You are asking God for a huge miracle. Charlyne and I want to do everything possible to see your family restored. Even though a trademark of Rejoice Marriage Ministries is to not give direct advice, today I feel led to break from that mold because of the magnitude of the problem and because of the potential future harm to your family. I want to offer some items for you to use as a checklist in staying away from becoming a situational stander.

- Wear your wedding band. That is a reminder to you and to all who come near you that you are a married person. That one action resolves many issues. (For centuries Catholic nuns, who never marry, have worn wedding bands as a symbol of their marriage to God. Should you do less?)

- Stay away from singles' ministries. This is where many people shop for future spouses and you are not eligible! You can find good fellowship and teaching elsewhere in your church or community, apart from a singles' ministry. Remember, in God's eyes, you are married.

- Have prayer partners of your same sex. Praying together brings about a level of intimacy. Save that for your returned spouse.

- Avoid phone chats with the opposite sex. If you are doing this, you are asking for trouble.

- Do not share details of your life or stand with the opposite sex.

- Do not go out, for any reason, with persons of the opposite sex, except in a large group. How would your prodigal spouse feel if someone reported seeing you out with a person of the opposite sex?

- If you feel led to call someone to see how they are doing, make it someone of the same sex.

- Avoid the "But we're just friends" syndrome. I recently heard a pastor say that if a person is voicing those words, they are already in trouble!

- Use as a guide the question, "If my spouse was home, would I be doing this?" For example, I would not go out for coffee with an opposite sex stander. So if you consider yourself married in God's eyes, why should you now?

- Stay out of unmonitored chat rooms. Limit the information you share with anyone online. (You do not know their sex, or even who they really are.) Limit email to the opposite sex to only what is absolutely necessary.

- Allow God to be your spouse, your companion, your friend not a person of the opposite sex, and not your computer.

- Look for opportunities to minister to people of the same sex, not the opposite sex.

- Avoid "I'll tell you my troubles if you'll tell me yours" scenarios with the opposite sex.

- Do not even think about what kind of husband or wife someone else would make.

- Do not look for loopholes allowing male/female relationships. Strive to see how far from the edge you can live. Refocus your thoughts, energies, time, and emotions on living as a married Christian, always striving to advance Kingdom work.

The bottom line is that every man and woman, who is serious about standing, needs to start considering themselves to be a married person in every way, from this day forward.

There is good news for you today. Regardless of how far you have strayed from being a stander and living a married lifestyle, there is forgiveness to be found in Jesus Christ. My prayer is that today you will seek His forgiveness, and also that you will make the changes needed in your life to live for Christ as one excited about His promise of marriage restoration.

God has something very special for you, in a healed marriage, with everyone serving Him. Charlyne and I desire to share with you any and every obstacle to restoration. The male/female issue is tough, but we sense it is an avoidable pitfall holding back marriage restoration.

THE "DOW" OF STANDING

"Do not store up for yourselves treasures on earth, where moth and rust destroy, and where thieves break in and steal. But store up for yourselves treasures in heaven, where moth and rust do not destroy, and where thieves do not break in and steal." **Matthew 6:19-20**

Even though Charlyne and I own no stock, it is interesting to hear the Dow Jones Average reported on the news each evening. It is amazing how insignificant events can cause the Dow to either plummet or rise. For example, last week a representative of Google mentioned in an interview their company's earnings for the period might not be as high as first announced. People began to buy and sell stock feverishly until the Dow had dropped over 100 points for that day.

Isn't it strange how a casual comment about one stock can have an effect on an entire stock market? In a way, that reminds me of standers who allow a casual comment by one person to have an effect on the value of their marriage and eventually the outcome of an entire family.

How is the "Dow" of your stand for marriage restoration? Is it strong, as you stand without wavering, waiting in confidence for God to do what He has promised? You must learn to toss off the negative comments from others.

The bottom line must be: Who are you allowing to set the value of your marriage? Do you allow God to tell you the importance of your family, during time spent in the Bible and prayer? Do you focus on the promises He has given you and the signs that He continues to show you? The alternative is that you are allowing people to set your "Dow" for you. You have heard from God directly about your marriage. The world will tell you, "They have their own free will" or "God has someone better" or "Get on with your life." This is not God's way. The only question must be what is God saying to you?

No owner of a thriving business wakes up one morning and suddenly announces, "I think today I will close the doors on my business." The people who close businesses are proprietors who have been sinking into trouble for a while. They have seen hints at business failure coming at them for a time, but did not take the needed corrective action to prevent a failure.

Right now without your spouse, you are the CEO of one of the most important businesses in the world: your family. If the mom and pop store down the street closed, lives would be changed, but people would recover. If you allow your marriage to sink, not depending totally on the restoration help that God has for you, the future of generations of your family could be forever changed.

Since we are comparing your marriage to a business, let's be very practical and look at two different family-operated gas stations that have gone out of business. The first station remains untouched for years. Windows are broken, weeds grow high, paint peels, and every month the property looks worse. At the second, a huge sign proclaims "Opening Soon." The station's grass is manicured, and the building maintained just as it was when open for business.

Which station do you predict will one day be demolished, and which can you see pumping gas again? If we can distinguish between prosperous and failing businesses, why is it so difficult to detect when a stand for marriage restoration is headed for trouble?

Men and women who seem to suddenly give up standing and praying for a prodigal mate are like the owner of a failing business. The signs were all there, but Satan might have had them blinded to what was happening. I want to share with you some indicators that might be present when the "Dow" on your stand may be dropping:

- You become so busy that something has to give. First to go is your devotional time and your time alone with the Lord.

- You listen to the opinions of others more than you listen to our Lord God.

- A favorite comment has become, "I don't see any change." (Remember, faith is believing where we cannot see a thing.)

- You allow the enemy to bring tiredness to you. Instead of planning how you can get rested, you fold up your stand.

- You still subscribe to marriage restoration newsletters, but you no longer read them very often.

- You no longer listen to your collection of CDs and read the books about God's miracle of marriage restoration. (Where you once were thrilled to receive a new CD, and almost wore it out in the first week, new CD now sits unopened.)

- Your wedding band is temporarily removed, for a good reason, but then never goes back on your hand.

- Personal head knowledge of standing exceeds your heart knowledge of walking daily with Jesus, allowing Him to guide you.

- You allow the line between the sacred and the secular to no longer exist.

- You think (or say), "This is too hard." (All you are doing is living a married lifestyle, while you become more like Jesus, praying for Him to touch your prodigal. If that is too hard, your Dow may be about to crash).

- You start to fantasize about specific people of the opposite sex.

- The email you send is more about the bad circumstances than about what God has promised to you.

- The computer replaces your Bible and you are spending more time online than in local church activities. (No, they are not the same.)

- You unintentionally emphasize the faults of your spouse to justify your own actions.

- You define "stander" as anyone wishing they had a spouse at home. (We use that name to describe a group of men and women, sold out to Jesus Christ, "standing" with Him, and praying to Him for the miracle of marriage restoration His way, regardless of the circumstances.)

- It is easier to talk about a far-off God than to tell others about your personal relationship with your Lord and Savior Jesus Christ.

- You become bitter and judgmental over the marriage restoration of others. You cannot rejoice in their miracles.

- You are more concerned with your personal happiness than with your personal holiness. (Does the Word say God wants you to be holy or happy?)

- Your prodigal mate's eternal destiny falls off the radar screen. Forgiveness becomes something for others, not for your prodigal.

- You no longer pray for the other person your spouse is involved with.

- You justify your actions and reactions, which are not based on the Word of God, but on the world's standards and the opinions of people.

- You feel comfortable having phone chats and talking online with people of the opposite sex.

- You go out with the opposite sex, but pass it off as "only coffee with a friend."

- When there is a crisis, you run to people and the computer, instead of running to God in prayer.

- You spend more time requesting prayer than you do actually praying.

- You have become comfortable with your single lifestyle.

- You look for encouragement from people, instead of asking God for special verses from His Word.

- You are no longer certain that you even want your prodigal home.

The "Dow" of a stand starts to fall when a strong stander forgets where the line between light and darkness lies. They become more comfortable with the world's solutions than with God's ways. Left unchecked, that line will totally disappear.

"This is the verdict: Light has come into the world, but men loved darkness instead of light because their deeds were evil." John 3:19

When the "Dow" of a stand begins to fall and nothing is done to change it, the person who once prayed so faithfully will wake up one day and realize their entire stand has vaporized. Many go on to other relationships, which they will later call a "painful detour." Some will later get back on track to re-build their stand.

When we were divorced and Charlyne was standing and praying for me, she must have had her moments when she wondered, "Why am I doing this?" but I never knew about them. I thank God that He gave me a praying, standing wife, with her priorities in order, and who worked at keeping her personal "Dow" closing higher every day. That, my friend, is how marriages are restored!

REPORTING ON STANDING

But the wisdom that comes from heaven is first of all pure; then peace-loving, considerate, submissive, full of mercy and good fruit, impartial and sincere. **James 3:17**

Have you ever wondered how newspapers, television and radio stations gather all the facts for the stories they report to us daily? A reporter with an inquisitive mind sets out to determine the facts. Each story we see or hear answers six critical questions:

Who? What? When? Where? Why? How?

Can you imagine the fallout if a television news anchor sat before the cameras at 6:00 P.M. and reported nothing more than, *"Someone told me. . ."or "I heard that. . ."* What if that man or woman interpreted what they had heard added their own view and reported it as fact? Thankfully, that is not the way it is done. Before the anchor gives you the answer to those six questions, an army of reporters, photographers, editors, producers, directors and fact checkers have done their work, so that the questions are answered as accurately as possible. Many times the information came from the PIO, or public information officer for an agency or organization. That individual has the responsibility of relaying accurate and timely information to media reporters.

While it takes a core of professional people to get the news out correctly, a man or woman standing for marriage restoration is often willing to accept the opinion of another individual as being the final word on a specific issue related to marriage/divorce/remarriage. Too often we witness individuals who appoint themselves the PIO for divorce and remarriage. They deliver their personal opinion as biblical fact, when in Truth, the Bible never specifically addresses the issue for which they have established rules. We hear a Scripture verse, or part of a verse, quoted as proof of their position, when a study of that Scripture and other verses surrounding it, as well as verses cross-referenced to it, do not support the position being attributed to it.

"If you then, though you are evil, know how to give good gifts to your children, how much more will your Father in heaven give the Holy Spirit to those who ask him!" **Luke 11:13**

The Bible is very clear and understandable that God hates divorce.

"I hate divorce," says the LORD God of Israel, "and I hate a man's covering himself with violence as well as with his garment," says the LORD Almighty. So guard yourself in your spirit, and do not break faith. **Malachi 2:16**

It is also clear that God's best is one man married to one woman for a lifetime.

Then the LORD God made a woman from the rib he had taken out of the man, and he brought her to the man. The man said, "This is now bone of my bones and flesh of my flesh; she shall be called 'woman,' for she was taken out of man." For this reason a man will leave his father and mother and be united to his wife, and they will become one flesh. **Genesis 2:22-24**

The Bible leaves many issues and situations open to interpretation. Some theologians have said this was intentional, with God knowing the tangled lives that many of His children would live before coming to know Jesus Christ as Lord and Savior.

How then, should an abandoned man or woman know God's plan for their marriage? They should ask Him (not others) and seriously seek His will for them. God's will is generalized that He hates divorce. His perfect will is also customized, especially for you.

You would be quite a sight if I had a suit custom made, or Charlyne had a dress custom made, (which we don't!) and then attempted to dictate that you had to wear our clothing. We know from Genesis and fig leaves in the Garden that God's will is for us to be clothed. Apart from a few general Old Testament references to clothing, God leaves it up to each of us to dress within His boundaries of moderation and decency.

If you won't accept our custom clothing, why accept the custom marriage and divorce opinions of someone else? Charlyne and I are asking you to become a reporter for standing and search out **who, what, when, where, why, and how** answers for yourself, not simply take our word nor the word of any other human. We are sinful. Why not ask your sinless God and Creator for His answers and direction to the hard questions of standing?

- **WHO** - *Who can stand for their marriage? I was married previously. Can I stand? My spouse is in a non-covenant marriage. Can I stand?*

- **WHAT** – *What is standing? Do I contact my prodigal spouse? I am being sued for divorce. Can I go to an attorney? Should I seek the counseling that I feel I need? What material do I need to purchase to stand? What if no one supports my stand?*

- **WHEN** - *When is God going to move? How long do I stand? When should I find someone else? When will my marriage be restored?*

- **WHERE** - *Where should I live while standing? Where should my tithe go? Where should I attend church alone? Where should I seek support while standing?*

- **WHY** - *Why is restoration taking so long? Why should I stand?*

- **HOW** - *How can God ever fix this mess we are in? How can God touch my spouse's hard heart? How will I ever make it alone? How could I ever stand for a long time?*

As a reporter for standing, you have two choices on where to find your answers. You could go to the Internet and find a multitude of people willing to answer each of the above questions for you, for the price of some material or a counseling fee. You then would be wearing their custom clothing, which may or may not fit you. Along with that, you could spend all day in "prayer" rooms and chat rooms, sharing all of your mate's faults and the circumstances with others, who will gladly hand you their custom clothing.

If any of you lacks wisdom, he should ask God, who gives generously to all without finding fault, and it will be given to him. But when he asks, he must believe and not doubt, because he who doubts is like a wave of the sea, blown and tossed by the wind. **James 1:5-6**

The better option–the only real option–is to go to God. Draw near to Him and ask Him your questions. If you have a right relationship with the Lord, Charlyne and I can assure you that He will answer you, guide you, correct you, provide for you and protect you.

When a reporter arrives at the scene of a huge disaster, (you may have a disaster at home today), that reporter does not go around grabbing bits and pieces from anyone who will talk to them. They first go to the PIO (public information officer) and get the facts. Afterward, they may interview people, but everything they see or hear is tested against the truth the PIO provided.

For answers to questions about your stand for restoration, we encourage you to turn away from the self-appointed PIO, who is attempting to convince you they have all the answers for their way of standing. Instead of a PIO who may have everything wrong, turn to and listen to God, who will always have everything right.

Our desire for your family is to see your spouse return home, once and for all, and for everyone in your family to come to Christ, serving Him, loving Him and depending on Him for your answers. It is our prayer that you will start living that way today. Stop listening to people, and start listening to God and see what a difference it will make in you, in your stand and then, in God's timing, in your prodigal spouse.

Reporters always work against deadlines. As a stander, you are facing two deadlines. Above all else, if your prodigal spouse dies in their sin, without Christ, they are going to Hell for all eternity. That is the cold, hard fact that should motivate you to stand for marriage restoration and family salvation.

"But I will show you whom you should fear: Fear him who, after the killing of the body, has power to throw you into hell. Yes, I tell you, fear him." **Luke 12:5**

Your second deadline is the moment your absent spouse walks back in the door. Right then, your stand goes "on the air." If you have not learned how to go to God alone for answers to your questions, you may have a mate back home, but with the same problems as before they exited. God wants to put a new heart in you and in your spouse. That happens when people listen to Him for their direction.

The heart of the discerning acquires knowledge; the ears of the wise seek it out. **Proverbs 18:15**

BE MORE CONSIDERATE

Husbands, in the same way be considerate as you live with your wives, and treat them with respect as the weaker partner and as heirs with you of the gracious gift of life, so that nothing will hinder your prayers. **I Peter 3:7**

Would you believe the Steinkamps have strife? At times it seems that the enemy is going around our home, looking for an open door, or even a crack, to get in. We work hard at keeping our home Satan proof. Nevertheless, just like every marriage, Charlyne and I have moments just like every couple that, left unchecked, could escalate into something far more serious.

One of the concepts we strive to teach standers is that there are no perfect, restored marriages, and yours will not be the first. After your prodigal returns, you need to expect times when things are less than perfect. You also need to prepare now for those times. These "moments of intense fellowship" will be ended in the prayer closet. There will be no winner or loser, unless you elect to play the "nothing's changed" card. Then Satan wins and your marriage is dealt one more blow.

Early one morning I was reading 1 Peter, one of my favorite books of the Bible. It was not intended, but I ended up in chapter 3, verse 7. Have you ever had God use a single word of Scripture to get you focused on what should be? That morning He used "considerate" from that verse to give me a reminder of my role in our marriage. It was not a reminder as much as it was a "workin' over," as my Kentucky relatives would say.

Last week I had a simple medical procedure done. Before the doctor started, I had to sign a release. It outlined what would be done and the results the treatment should bring about. The form also listed potential side effects which ranged from redness at the injection site to death. If anyone read that list and did not understand these were remote possibilities, they would not consent to the procedure. I understood what all could happen and signed the form. This week I have a mild infection at a previous injection site on my knee. The doctor told me how to treat it. Never was amputating my leg considered.

By the same measure, we hear of a marriage where a prodigal spouse has returned. Often no one is giving the marriage time to heal. At the first small sign of redness or soreness, someone wants to amputate that marriage once again.

Even though the Bible addresses 1 Peter 3:7 only to husbands, this is being written for husbands and wives. Neither sex has an exclusive on being considerate to their spouse. This is also being written to both standers and to returned prodigals. My prayer is that you can comprehend the spiritual battle that is taking place for your marriage.

Ephesians, chapter 2, explains what has happened:

As for you, you were dead in your transgressions and sins, in which you used to live when you followed the ways of this world and of the ruler of the kingdom of the air, the spirit who is now at work in those who are disobedient. All of us also lived among them at one time, gratifying the cravings of our sinful nature and following its desires and thoughts. Like the rest, we were by nature objects of wrath. But because of his great love for us, God, who is rich in mercy, made us alive with Christ even when we were dead in transgressions it is by grace you have been saved.
Ephesians 2:1-5

I used one of my wife's favorite Bible study techniques and cross referenced the word "considerate." I discovered that Titus, chapter 3 could have been written to standers and prodigals alike, both before and after marriage restoration:

Our Warrant -

Remind the people to be subject to rulers and authorities, to be obedient, to be ready to do whatever is good, to slander no one, to be peaceable and considerate, and to show true humility toward all men. ***Titus 3:1-2***

God's Word has warranted, or commanded, each of us to not only be subject to authority, but to be peaceable and considerate, showing humility. Could He have meant toward our spouses, regardless of what they have done?

Our Waywardness -

At one time we too were foolish, disobedient, deceived and enslaved by all kinds of passions and pleasures. We lived in malice and envy, being hated and hating one another. ***Titus 3:3***

Regardless of how dark any of our paths have been, once we come to Jesus, confessing and believing accepting His free gift of eternal life, our past becomes as clean as fresh snow. As a character in one of my fiction stories sings, "It matters not how dark your past has been, let the blood of Jesus cover all that sin."

Our Wonder -

But when the kindness and love of God our Savior appeared, he saved us, not because of righteous things we had done, but because of his mercy. He saved us through the washing of rebirth and renewal by the Holy Spirit, whom he poured out on us generously through Jesus Christ our Savior, so that, having been justified by his grace, we might become heirs having the hope of eternal life. ***Titus 3:4-7***

The Bible refers to this as a "mystery," that Jesus, the one without sin, dying on a cross, shed His blood to pay for my sin. It is also a mystery how this forgiving grace is available to even the worst sinner right now.

Our Willingness -

This is a trustworthy saying. And I want you to stress these things, so that those who have trusted in God may be careful to devote themselves to doing what is good. These things are excellent and profitable for everyone. **Titus 3:8**

Are you willing to devote yourself to doing what is good, or do you still seek revenge for what your spouse has done? Which way will be "excellent and profitable for everyone?" Which way will open the door for marriage restoration?

Our Warning -

But avoid foolish controversies and genealogies and arguments and quarrels about the law, because these are unprofitable and useless. **Titus 3:9**

Satan loves to see God's children get caught up in unprofitable and useless debate, not only with a spouse, but also with fellow Christians. On that day when we each stand before God, there is only going to be one question with eternal significance, "What have you done with Jesus?" The question of who was right and who was wrong on any issue will not matter much right then.

Our Way -

Our people must learn to devote themselves to doing what is good, in order that they may provide for daily necessities and not live unproductive lives. **Titus 3:14**

In this verse God calls us to do what is good. Since He hates divorce, doing good must include standing with Him for our marriage restoration. To the prodigal, doing well would mean repenting of sin and going home to a waiting spouse. To everyone, it clearly commands us to provide for our daily necessities and not live unproductive lives. Even though a productive life means working at what God has called us to do, it also means sharing by both word and example that we serve a Lord who heals hurting marriages.

Well, where are you? For me, I have been taught my lesson anew that God wants me to be considerate of everyone from my wife to the stranger in traffic that I will never see again.

One of the goals of this ministry is to share ways that God can change you so that your spouse will be asking, "What's different about him/her?" One of the greatest changes is for you to become more considerate of everyone. That's the way marriages are restored, to the glory of God.

For where you have envy and selfish ambition, there you find disorder and every evil practice. But the wisdom that comes from heaven is first of all pure; then peace-loving, considerate, submissive, full of mercy and good fruit, impartial and sincere. Peacemakers who sow in peace raise a harvest of righteousness. **James 3:16-18**

18 SIGNS THAT SOMETHING IS HAPPENING!

For our struggle is not against flesh and blood, but against the rulers, against the authorities, against the powers of this dark world and against the spiritual forces of evil in the heavenly realms. **Ephesians 6:12**

During my prodigal days, while we were divorced, I heard a pastor make a sermon statement that has stuck with me to this day: "If you were able to see the spiritual battle that is taking place all around you, it would scare you to death." My spiritual eyes were not yet opened, so I could not fully understand what that respected man of God was saying, but nevertheless, I remembered.

Since standing with God for marriage restoration is a spiritual battle, you may not recognize the back and forth of Satan's ways as God's will is being performed. I want to share with you some of the ways that you can know something is happening in the heavenly realms.

It is not necessary for all eighteen ways to be seen for your spouse to be brought home, nor will they happen in any specific order. You may even see your prodigal coming up the walk before you see any of these signs; most likely some of these things will be happening:

- You feel like giving up. The enemy will make you think nothing is happening and nothing will ever change.

- You start to sense an increased burden for your prodigal's soul. The restoration of your marriage does not seem nearly as important as where your beloved will spend eternity.

- The Lord burdens you to pray for your husband or wife at the strangest times. For some people, God awakens them during the night to pray.

- Satan sends a counterfeit into your life. Just when things are the bleakest, Mr. Right or Miss Perfect arrives. Some standers make the mistake of thinking, "This must be of God because we are so perfectly suited for each other." Counterfeits always look better than the real thing.

- People are constantly reminding you about your mate's free will and how you have grounds for divorce.

- People tell you God wants you to be "happy." In truth, God is a lot more concerned about your holiness than He is about your happiness. He also cares about your mate's lost condition.

- You can see no way out of specific circumstances, such as financial problems. Remember, God works best when nothing else will.

- You are tempted to take off your wedding ring.

- You find Scripture that seems to have been written just for you. The Word speaks to your heart and to your needs.

- Some of the actions of your prodigal spouse are unexplainable. For example, I repeatedly asked Charlyne to stop praying for me. I just knew the conviction that I was under came as a result of her prayers.

- The enemy can even use your family members to dissuade you when the spiritual battle is the hottest. An older teen may say, "If he/she is allowed back, I am going." Your parents may become dead set against restoration. Do not allow this to discourage you. Over the years, we have been witnesses time and time again of God restoring family relationships as well as marriages.

- You mistakenly start to view your local church as a hindrance to restoration. Satan may give you fear over how your returned prodigal would fit in. Your pastor may come out against marriage restoration. The returned spouse and their church relationship is one of the many areas that God can and does heal for restoring families. Right now, you need the love and support of a church family.

- Prayer partners may be removed. There came a time in Charlyne's stand, near the day of our remarriage and before the Internet, when my wife's personal prayer partner moved out-of-state. God was telling my wife that she needed to depend on Him, not others.

- Major changes in your prodigal mate's life are happening. For some, this is a new job. For others, it is relocation to a distant state, making restoration seem even more impossible. There may be the attempted legalizing of adultery through a marriage license, or a non-covenant child is born.

- You are tempted to make major changes in your own life. It could be reclaiming your maiden name or changing the door locks on your home for no reason. Whatever you are considering doing, it would say to your prodigal spouse, "It's over!"

- You sense a certain uneasiness in your spirit. Where you had once started growing in the Lord as a stander, you now feel something indescribable in your life. Some people confuse God wanting them to intensify their stand with Him, with God wanting them to give up on their stand for a healed home.

- You can forgive your prodigal spouse, even to the extent that you have pity for them, for how deceived they are, and for the situations they are in.

- Your prodigal makes false starts toward home or toward family events, and then just as suddenly withdraws or backs out.

Do you get it? Some of these signs are negative and some are positive. Together, they allow you to catch a glimpse of the battle that is raging in the heavenlies. This battle is for much more than your marriage. It is for your prodigal's eternal soul, and for future generations of your family.

The number one mistake that men and women praying for marriage restoration make is attempting to do spiritual battle with earthly weapons, based on earthly reasoning. They do not understand that spiritual battles, such as the one they are in, can be won only by using spiritual weapons. They use the courts instead of compassion, seeking revenge instead of restoration. They want to heap guilt on the absent spouse instead of grace. Instead of covering their prodigal's nakedness and shame, they want to broadcast it. Walking with Jesus, they become better. Walking in the world's way, they will only become bitter.

The change we see in successful standers is amazing. Somewhere along the way to marriage restoration, the spiritual lights come on, and the stander realizes they are in a spiritual battle. They start to do war against the enemy, and not against their spouse. They may have their ups and downs, but overall, a steady growth in the things of God is noted until their prodigal comes home to both them and to their Lord. May you stand strong until that grand day.

THERE'S NO PLACE LIKE HOME

"Then we your people, the sheep of your pasture, will praise you forever; from generation to generation we will recount your praise." **Psalm 79:13**

During my prodigal days when all three of our children were still school age, I never considered what life would be like a couple decades in the future, when we had grandchildren. If I had continued on the road Satan wanted for me, my relationship with my grandchildren would be strained, at the very least. We know of prodigals who are not allowed to see their grandchildren at all.

If I had married some other woman, she would probably have children and eventually grandchildren, so she would expect me to be a step-grandfather to those children, though I had no blood relation to them. I might be spending time with the other woman's adult children, who wanted their other father to be a grandfather to their kids, and not me.

On the other hand, if Charlyne had given up on her stand and married another man that would be his relationship to my grandchildren. I am certain that Charlyne would be seeing a few Steinkamp traits in our grandchildren, each one reminding her of me and making her wonder what her life could have been like if she had not given up praying for me.

There could be some other man sitting in my recliner. Instead of having a grandpa our grandkids have known all their lives, a man who had somehow dropped into our family would be attempting to love their grandma. It is doubtful if those seven precious grandchildren would ever come to know him well enough to share the things with him that they share with me.

All seven of our grandchildren have already lost a grandparent on the other side of their family to death. Why would I want to hurt them even more by choosing to drop out of their lives, replacing the role God gave me with my selfish and sinful attempts at happiness?

My own Grandpa Lee was close to me in my early years. On most Saturdays I could be found doing whatever Grandpa Lee was doing. When I was in the fourth or fifth grade, Grandpa Lee abandoned my grandma for another woman. I was devastated, and our relationship was never the same again. About 30 years later, my grandpa finally repented for what he had done, sobbing over my grandmother's casket at the cemetery. He begged his daughters to forgive him while the other woman stood awkwardly in the background.

The entire divorce issue is a mess, disadvantaging not only spouses and children for life, but also grandchildren. And that is just the tip of the iceberg. If you could read the letters and email we receive, you would hate divorce as much as we do. "Divorce recovery" is an oxymoron because there is no recovering from divorce.

I wish every prodigal, or even every potential prodigal, could have two views into the future: one of how they and their family might be in 25 years if they came to Christ, stayed at home and lived for Him; the other of how their own life, their spouse, their children and their grandchildren might be in 25 years, if they continue on the road to another spouse and forsaking their own family.

God does not issue crystal balls to families in trouble. He gives something much better, if each of us would only accept it. He gives faith to the standing spouse in a struggling marriage. By faith they can see their marriage restored by God. Their faith is not diminished because they understand it will not happen in an instant. Through faith, the stander stops depending on their spouse. They stop depending on what they can do and start depending on what

God can do to heal their marriage. Most of all, faith allows them to depend on what God has promised to them.

It has taken Charlyne and me almost 45 years to build the family of fifteen that we enjoy today. How could I have ever thought that I could bail out, find someone else and that the Steinkamp family would thrive to be the close unit that it is today? That does not happen.

One Friday evening our son Tom was on call and his wife was going to a ladies' party, so we had six-year-old Samantha for the evening. Although we enjoy being around all seven of our grandchildren at once, the time we spend with one grandchild at a time is so very special

Charlyne gave Sam her bath and shampooed her hair. I suspect that Charlyne reminded Sam she was in the same tub that her daddy had bathed in when he was that age. All of our grandkids delight in hearing about the stability of their grandparents being in one place for a long time.

Our home may be small and outdated, but I would not trade it for the two-story mansion almost completed next to us. We bought our home in 1966 when we married. We made additions twice when another child was on the way. I have told Charlyne the only way I will leave this home is feet first.

When Madison's hamster died, she told her dad, Tim, she wanted it buried in our back yard since we will always be here. In fact, there is almost a pet cemetery out back with our children's deceased pets, and now our grandchildren's.

I attempted to move out of this home once. It took going through a divorce and much more, but one day God stopped gently guiding me toward home, as He had done for almost my entire prodigal journey. That July day God pointed me toward home and said, "Enough is enough." I sense in my spirit that if I had not returned home that day

God would have said, "You are embarrassing me, calling yourself a Christian but living a life of sin," and would have taken my life.

In our home, there is a small nail behind my recliner where each grandchild used to hang large plastic keys when they were at the keys stage of crawling. Everyone knows where each Christmas item plugs in, as well as which circuit breaker to flip when the lights in my office go out. When we are preparing for a hurricane, regardless of who comes to help us secure everything, they know where everything goes. This place is our home.

All three of our adult children still have keys to our home, as do their spouses. All six know they are welcome here, without knocking, at any time. Our home has always been the perfect spot for everything from changing a diaper to changing a ball uniform. Our home is part bus station, where sleepover and after school kids are passed between parents. The grandkids know where grandma keeps the good snacks. That second generation swings on the opened refrigerator door, looking for nothing special but taking inventory, just like their parents did 20 or 30 years ago.

We hear from standers who are concerned that because of divorce, there is no longer a home where God can restore their marriage. For some, their home was sold as part of the divorce settlement. Others have lost the family home through foreclosure. Others have sold their home and moved out of their area. Regardless of where you live, God knows your address. Even if you do not have a clue where your prodigal might be, God knows. The Lord also knows the exact place where He will rebuild a home for you and for your spouse or family.

On the day we remarried, I would have gone home with Charlyne, even if she had to live in her car in the parking lot of the doctor's office where she worked. It is the love that you are asking Jesus to rebuild that can make any place a home, be it an oceanfront mansion or a hotel room. It is a lie from the enemy, pure and simple, that God cannot restore your marriage because you no longer have a family home. Please do not buy into that illogical reasoning.

Other standers or their spouses have declared bankruptcy. Someone is concerned they will never be able to afford to buy a home because of their credit. Leave that up to God for the days ahead. Do not worry about it today.

Over the years Charlyne and I have known standers who lived in the most humble surroundings, yet they managed to make it their home. When God had everyone ready, their spouse would have been honored to live with them in that location. On the day you and your prodigal reunite, your beloved will be much more interested in your love and forgiveness than in your decor.

What will your prodigal be looking for? A place of peace. When we come out of the roar and confusion of the far country, we only want a place of peace. It is really the peace of God we are seeking, but many prodigals, including this one, equate the peace at home with the peace of God. Since you do not know when your spouse will appear, it is important to make your home, regardless of where it might be right now, a place of peace.

When Charlyne left for work on the Wednesday morning we remarried, she ushered three kids out the door to camp without any idea she would return home eight hours later a married woman with a returned prodigal close on her heels. As I re-entered our home, I did not stumble over a mountain of clothes. When I went into our bedroom and called the other woman to inform her I had come home to my family, I sat on a bed that was made. Charlyne did not have to run ahead of me to move anything she did not want me to see. Even though I had no belongings with me, I saw that my part of the closet was empty - except for a wedding dress. I do not know how Charlyne managed to keep everything done, but I cannot recall Charlyne uttering an "I was going to . . ." apology about anything that evening.

That's enough about what your prodigal may be looking for in a home. There is something that needs to be more important to you right now. What is God looking for in a home inside you? He is looking for a pure heart, with sins forgiven, where His Spirit might dwell. Once that internal home is cleaned and ready, get ready for your external house to be turned into a home, by the power of God.

I pray that out of his glorious riches he may strengthen you with power through his Spirit in your inner being, so that Christ may dwell in your hearts through faith. And I pray that you, being rooted and established in love, may have power, together with all the saints, to grasp how wide and long and high and deep is the love of Christ, and to know this love that surpasses knowledge-that you may be filled to the measure of all the fullness of God. **Ephesians 3:16-19**

Bob and his father, 1950.

The Steinkamp family prior to the divorce.

One of Bob's prodigal homes.

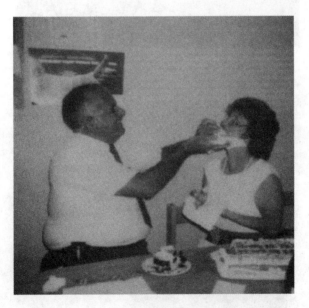

July 7, 1987

Bob and Charlyne's wedding picture at an impromptu
reception at Charlyne's office following their sudden
remarriage.

Bob and Charlyne on their second honeymoon.

Bob and Frances, Rejoice Marriage Ministries first
intercessor.

Home, sweet, home!

The Steinkamp family.

Bob and Charlyne sharing at a Rejoice Pompano Bible Study.

Bob and Charlyne's family at Bob's funeral service.

Easter 2011
Charlyne and her grandchildren.

Bob and Charlyne

TO BE LIKE JESUS

Whoever claims to live in him must walk as Jesus did.
1 John 2:6

What is the answer for direction in your stand for a restored marriage? You need to seek and discover God's plan for your family, where He is working, and then meet Him there. How is that accomplished? By you being like Jesus, in as many ways as possible.

How about striving to make your life and your stand like Jesus? No better example ever walked this earth than Him. Jesus led a sinless life. He never made a mistake. He answered every challenge correctly. In many ways, He was the first and the ultimate "Stander," sacrificing His very life for each of us individually.

But for that very reason I was shown mercy so that in me, the worst of sinners, Christ Jesus might display his unlimited patience as an example for those who would believe on him and receive eternal life. Now to the King eternal, immortal, invisible, the only God, be honor and glory for ever and ever. Amen.   I Timothy 1:16-17

"I have set you an example that you should do as I have done for you. I tell you the truth, no servant is greater than his master, nor is a messenger greater than the one who sent him." John 13:15-16

Today, tomorrow, and every day, you can be like Jesus in so many ways:

- **Be like Jesus in your steps** - We each can walk the way that Jesus walked, being careful where we go, and going out of our way to minister to God's hurting children.

- **Be like Jesus in your speech** - How did Jesus talk? Did His words hurt or help? May each of us speak (and send our email) according to the example of the Master.

- **Be like Jesus in your sacrifice** - How much are you willing to give up for another? Do you hurt when you observe someone else hurting, or do you turn away with indifference? Are you giving back to the Lord His tithe (10%) through your local church?

- **Be like Jesus in your standards** - Are your ethics and values rooted and grounded in the Word of God, or do your standards change according to your surroundings? Jesus never changes.

- **Be like Jesus in your service** - Are you supporting with your service the church and ministries that are supporting you? Do you have God-given talents that should be put to use in Kingdom building?

- **Be like Jesus in your stand** - Jesus did not have to die for the sins of each of us. He loved us with an unconditional love, not allowing us to receive the punishment from God that we deserved. Do you love your unlovable spouse with that same love, or is your love conditional upon their action?

The bottom line is not, *"Can you be like Jesus?"* but rather *"Do you want to be like Jesus?"* May each of us make it our goal each and every day to live in such a way as to be more like Jesus. Not only does your marriage and the salvation of family members depend on it, others are watching and copying you.

THE PRODIGAL'S GUILT AND SHAME

David was conscience-stricken after he had counted the fighting men, and he said to the LORD, "I have sinned greatly in what I have done. Now, O LORD, I beg you, take away the guilt of your servant. I have done a very foolish thing." **2 Samuel 24:10**

Charlyne and I receive many questions about the process of marriage restoration. Standers have trouble understanding what has happened when a prodigal spouse makes false starts toward coming home. The absent mate comes home, and then just as quickly leaves again, often becoming more distant than before. Some standers endure this cycle more than once before their mate stays home.

I decided to address two obstacles to coming home, as we prodigals see things. Those roadblocks are guilt and shame.

In the Scripture passage above, David was "conscience-stricken" over his sin. You may be thinking of David's sin of adultery with Bathsheba and having her husband killed in battle. That sin happened years before the sin mentioned in this verse. David was a very old man, and nearing the end of his life. What had caused David to feel so guilty that the Bible tells us he was sleepless? He had counted his troops wrong.

"Playing with the numbers was a sin?" Yes, and it still is today. I pray that today you can see David, a lad who slew Goliath and was later chosen by God to be the leader of his people. He committed adultery, caused a murder, and much more. David came back to God in repentance. Now near the end of his life, David is crying out to God, simply because he had played with the numbers.

Even though your prodigal spouse has never killed a giant, nor led a nation, the one you love may be at the Bathsheba stage of David's lifestyle today. Their sin is very open, and they seem to have no shame. My wife and I pray that by helping you to see where your prodigal really is right now, you can continue to stand and pray for their repentance, regardless of the timetable. Remember, God is always right on time.

Can you envision your returned prodigal, late in life, so sensitive to the things of God that they toss and turn at night over what some people would pass off as a "white" lie? Please allow me to explain.

Let's compare where your spouse is right now to the pendulum on an old grandfather clock. The farther the pendulum is pulled to one side, the farther to the other side it will go, but only when released. Your assignment is to pray for the release of your mate from the clutches of sin.

Restoration is a process that starts with coming home. That is the beginning, not the end. Yes, there are ups and downs as the prodigal grieves the absence of the other person, and you re-adjust to each other as husband and wife. There may be child issues, financial concerns and a hundred other things that always result in a trip to the pig pens of life. Above all else, know that the enemy will use every opportunity to destroy a restoring couple.

From my own experience and from talking with other men and women who are years into restored marriages, the consensus seems to be, "I'll never go there again." Could that be where David found himself in this passage? He recalled the trouble that earlier sin had caused him, and it frightened him.

Are you prepared to deal with your prodigal's guilt and shame when they come home? If not, you are not ready for restoration. When your prodigal utters, "I feel so ashamed," are you going to reply, "You should?" Or are you prepared to offer the comfort in Jesus that they will need?

Guilt and shame are powerful tools of Satan. They attempt to convince us prodigals that the journey home is impossible. No one can walk out on a family, regardless of the circumstances, and not feel guilty. We prodigals may have our shame masked for a season, but there will be a day in the restoration process when we must come face to face with what we have done.

After divorce, the other woman and I attended a large church that Charlyne and I had attended. One of the ushers had been a friend of ours. When I was with the other woman, that man would go out of his way to avoid meeting me in an aisle. In my sinful state, I enjoyed seeing him side-step into a pew to avoid having to greet me. Only after I had come home, did I realize how shameful my actions had been, and the position I had put that man in.

We need to look at the shame of the stander as well. There is one phrase I pray that you never utter. Never end a sentence with, ". . .after what you've put this family through," or any words even remotely close to that thought. If you are still harboring shame over what your mate has done, you are not ready for restoration. Release any shame to the Lord today.

Your prodigal may be viewing their guilt and shame as two huge walls blocking them from your home. Charlyne and I pray that you will be able to demolish those walls and pave the pathway home with your prayers. We want your prodigal to become like a David, so sensitive to you and to our God, that nothing damaging will be allowed into those two relationships.

Is that even possible? Not only is it possible, it is also probable. Today you may be facing what seems like huge obstacles. Your spouse and the other person might be co-workers. There may be ongoing contact between them. Nothing good will ever be accomplished by your spying, but all things are possible through your praying.

If you continue to stand strong, even after the prodigal returns, and take your counsel from God, not from people, there will come a day when your spouse realizes their full love, devotion, and attention belong at home, to be shared with a spouse and with God, not shared between a spouse and a counterfeit.

Charlyne and I are honored that we have prodigal spouses subscribed to these daily messages. As an aside to you, I promise that it is possible to get over that other person. The key is having absolutely no contact with the other person, for any reason, for six months. During that time, God will help you deal with the guilt and shame. The affection you feel now will diminish with time. On the other hand, each contact is like tossing gasoline into a fire. It is worth the pain to have your spouse and family back again.

You know my folly, O God; my guilt is not hidden from you. May those who hope in you not be disgraced because of me, O Lord, the LORD Almighty; may those who seek you not be put to shame because of me, O God of Israel. **Psalm 69:5-6**

"YOU SHALL NOT STEAL"

"You shall not steal." **Exodus 20:15**

One Monday evening we celebrated two birthdays at Rejoice Pompano Beach. On the way to class, Charlyne stopped at the supermarket to pick up the cake we had ordered. We have purchased cakes from that store for over 25 years. Until this trip, cakes were always picked up in the bakery department and paid for at the checkout before leaving the store.

On this trip, Charlyne was given a ticket and told she could pick up the cake after paying for it. The apologetic baker explained the new system was put in place after the store had over $1,000 worth of cakes stolen in one month. People stealing cakes destined for happy occasions? Can you imagine!

Many of the precepts for life that we follow are extracted from Holy Scripture. Some of these rules are surrounded by qualifiers, such as, "when" or "if." As you know, some of the passages related to marriage and divorce are open to interpretation. The passage we know as The Ten Commandments is not like that. The four words we are looking at today, "You shall not steal," are sitting all by themselves. There is no way anyone could read anything into this verse other than God's commanding each of us not to steal.

Why am I addressing not stealing with a group of men and women who are trusting God and praying for marriage restoration? Charlyne and I desire that every obstacle, regardless of how small, be removed from your life to allow God to do His mighty work in your marriage. To reach that point, on the topic of stealing, I may have to meddle a bit. May I do that?

What is the dictionary definition of steal? "To take something not rightfully belonging to one without its owner's consent, especially secretly." That does not leave much wiggle room, does it?

All of us will acknowledge that walking out of a busy supermarket without paying for a cake is stealing, but what about the more subtle temptations to steal that you and I face every day?

Jesus Himself repeated the command not to steal:

Now a man came up to Jesus and asked, "Teacher, what good thing must I do to get eternal life?" "Why do you ask me about what is good?" Jesus replied. "There is only One who is good. If you want to enter life, obey the commandments." "Which ones?" The man inquired. Jesus replied, "'Do not murder, do not commit adultery, do not steal, do not give false testimony, honor your father and mother,' and 'love your neighbor as yourself.'" **Matthew 19:16:19**

What could standers possibly be stealing? How about stealing whatever remnant is left of your prodigal mate's reputation?

My journey home was made easier by Charlyne's refusal to tell anyone who would listen all that she knew, or even what she suspected about my sinful mis-adventures. My wife has told me, and it has since been confirmed by others, that Charlyne used some standard phrases whenever anyone would ask, "How is Bob?" (Translated into Prodigalese, the language used by prodigals, such a statement usually means, "any new gossip or rumors about your husband that I can embellish and pass around the church?") Charlyne's reply might have been, "God is at work," or "Keep praying for him." I could walk back into church, because most people only knew that we had been divorced, and that God had brought us back together again.

Right now, I only need to go as far as the Ministry email to learn more about some prodigals than I want to know. Much of what would be recorded there would be rumors that a stander had heard. Thankfully, those emails never leave us. I could also go on the Internet right now and read page after page after page of prodigal-slamming comments, published for the world to read.

If you are seeking a rock-solid marriage restored by Jesus with each member loving and serving Him, and determined to never walk out again, you must follow my wife's advice; "Zip the lips."

The Proverbs amplify Charlyne's thought:

Through the blessing of the upright a city is exalted, but by the mouth of the wicked it is destroyed. A man who lacks judgment derides his neighbor, but a man of understanding holds his tongue. A gossip betrays a confidence, but a trustworthy man keeps a secret.
Proverbs 11:11-13

Marriage restoration God's way demands that you hold your tongue. Doing anything else would be stealing your prodigal's reputation. Do standers really steal? Let's look at some scenarios:

You have ten dollars to last a week. You buy five dollars' worth of gas, but the clerk gives you change for a twenty. Do you return it or do you justify that is God's way of blessing you?

Your employer observes you busy on the computer. They think you are working, but you are busy doing something else online. Are you stealing the company's time?

Your child needs paper for a school project. The office where you work has plenty, so you quietly slide a stack of

80

paper into your items going home. Is that stealing? Who bought the paper?

There is something online you really want, but do not have the money to purchase. A friend shares their password to the site and it works. Is that stealing from the website's owner?

Each of these illustrations could be justified away, but in each of our heart of hearts, we fully know when something is being stolen. If you need a more definite test to determine stealing, look at the dictionary definition, where "especially secretly" is noted. Could you tell the store clerk they gave you too much change, or allow the boss to know how much of your computer time or time at the copier is for personal work?

As stated before, Charlyne and I desire that you and every stander put aside every hindrance to your being 100% like Jesus in all that you do. If it is necessary for you to change your actions, your attitudes, and your talk so that the Lord can bring your spouse home, we pray that you will allow those changes to happen.

There is a second reason that I feel led to share with you about stealing. You are a victim of stealing. Someone, or some habit, has stolen your spouse. We can surely apply the dictionary "especially secretly" clause to your theft. Be it another person, alcohol, drugs, pornography, or any combination of these, it began in secret. What was once so secretive is now so public. At some point, stealing in private always becomes public.

If you are like most standers, people will attempt to steal even more from you this very day. The world will attempt to steal your hope for a marriage restored by God. You need to have Scripture ammunition ready for each and every "get on with your life" or "someone better" comment.

Your spouse has been stolen. It is my prayer that you will turn from being a victim to being a victor, by always living, always talking, and always acting like Jesus.

Therefore each of you must put off falsehood and speak truthfully to his neighbor, for we are all members of one body. "In your anger do not sin": Do not let the sun go down while you are still angry, and do not give the devil a foothold. He who has been stealing must steal no longer, but must work, doing something useful with his own hands, that he may have something to share with those in need.
Ephesians 4:25-28

THE ONE - MINUTE WINDOW

. . .Always be prepared to give an answer to everyone who asks you to give the reason for the hope that you have. But do this with gentleness and respect. **I Peter 3:15**

Would you take a quick quiz with me?

1) At the fast food drive-thru in your small town, you reach for your bag of burgers with your left hand, showing the wedding band you are wearing while standing. A friend handing you the order exclaims, "A wedding ring! Congratulations!" What do you do?

(A) Eat burgers from the same place for the next four meals so you can hand the person a CD explaining marriage restoration; (B) Block the window until you have told your story in detail; (C) Quote Scripture, which is not understood, to the employee; (D) Give your testimony of standing in only a few seconds.

2) Your church service has a time for people to greet one another. On a Sunday morning, the person sitting behind you shakes your hand and inquires, "What's this I hear about you waiting for your terrible spouse?" What do you do?

(A) Pass it off with, "We're going to divorce court in a few weeks and it will be over." (B) Gather up your things, move into the pew next to the person, and use sermon time to pass a series of notes explaining standing. (C) Promise to bring them a book, which you forget to do. (D) Give your testimony of standing in a few seconds.

3) On a beautiful summer day, you are sitting at a traffic light with your windows down. The passenger in the vehicle next to you noticed your *"God Heals Hurting Marriages"* bumper sticker and calls out, "You really think God heals marriages?" You could:

(A) Motion the driver to pull over, which they probably won't do, so you can explain your stand for half an hour. (B) Try to stay beside the car for the next ten blocks, shouting out your story. (C) Toss a restoration CD toward the other vehicle's open window. (D) Give your testimony of standing in only a few seconds.

Option D seems to be the correct answer in each scenario.

God is going to give every man and woman who is standing with Him for marriage restoration the opportunity, more than once, to share with both friends and strangers what He is doing. Are you prepared?

Done without books or CDs, no written notes, no time to look up a Bible verse, you need to work on being able to concisely praise God for healing families. It can happen in line at the bank, between classes at school, in a Sunday school discussion, or on the job with a co-worker.

Charlyne and I attended a conference. Between two sessions, I found myself alone with another man on a hotel elevator. He was eyeing my conference name tag.

"Marriage ministry? I keep seeing those name tags around here. What's it all about?"

I knew I had only the time between a few hotel floors to share my testimony. Before the door opened half a minute later, I had shared the Steinkamp story. I do not know the man and have not seen him since. I do not know if he was a Christian. What I shared could have been forgotten before the elevator doors closed, or it could have made an eternal difference in a family.

Here is basically what I said:

"We had a rough marriage for years. I was abusive and unfaithful. We wore masks on Sundays to our church.

Finally, my wife divorced me. I found someone else, but my wife took a stand with God, praying for the restoration of our marriage. Two years later we were remarried. Now God allows us to help other hurting couples discover that God heals hurting marriages."

The elevator doors opened, the man said, "Thank You," and disappeared. I asked God if I had done my best for Him in that unexpected situation. I pray that man took away from our meeting in an elevator a few highlights, such as: married long time with problems, going to church, divorced, and most important, God heals hurting marriages. There was no time, nor was there need to share the web address of a ministry or any details of our problems.

If you read the above testimony aloud, it will take less than 30 seconds. Do you realize how many one minute windows you have every day when the subject of marriage has come up?

God seems to give Charlyne or me an opportunity to use a one-minute restored marriage testimony at least once a week. It can be to a busy deliveryman who brings a package or to the parking valet who brought our car to the front of a medical office building.

God does not want you to wait until your marriage is restored to start testifying what He can do for a hurting family. Some standers are invited to give their testimony of hope in marriage restoration to a church group, but God is going to give every stander an equal amount of time, one minute at a time, to share what He is doing for their marriage. Will you be ready?

The advantages of using a one-minute testimony are many. Foremost, no one can minimize or criticize your personal experience. You do not need to have the person call you, nor meet with you. Since everything you share is in your heart, you are always prepared.

People often have trouble condensing their testimonies. The Rejoice webpage to which testimonies for Saturday are submitted, limits submissions to a few hundred words. We can only use brief excerpts. When we receive lengthy stories we may miss the most important points. Nevertheless, we hear from people who say they cannot tell their testimony in the space provided. We have had visitors at Rejoice Pompano who are invited to share a ten minute testimony and they say they need more time.

Do you realize any Christian testimony has only three main points that need to be shared?

1. What I was before. 2. Where I am now. 3. What God has done in my life.

A stander's one-minute testimony is an opportunity to exalt God, not to criticize your spouse. I am hesitant to use an example, for fear someone will take it as a form to use, but here is one example of how a stander might share a one minute testimony:

"After a few years of marriage, our first child died. My husband couldn't cope with his grief and turned to the vices of the world. We divorced. I was hurting so badly. A friend took me to church for the first time in years and I met Jesus. Now He is my best friend. God has shown me that He will restore my marriage. Right now I am standing with God and praying for my husband to discover how much Jesus loves him, just as I did."

That testimony takes about 30 seconds to deliver.

Standers tend to make two common mistakes in their short testimony. First, they want to put too much travel into their story, ("In 1984 we moved to Buffalo, or maybe it was 1985.") You need to finish within a minute, and have people remember only what a difference Jesus has made in your life, not that you once lived in Buffalo.

The second error that standers tend to make in their one-minute testimony is using words that a lost world does not understand. In fact, they can be turned off by them. The focus needs to be testifying about what Jesus is doing in your marriage in one minute. If you share Christian terminology, such as "being spirit filled," the average person outside the church has no idea what you mean.

This message will reach thousands of people in scores of nations. Can you imagine if every stander who reads this would polish their one-minute testimony and share it with only two people every day? Do you realize how fast the entire world could hear about marriage restoration, instead of caving in to divorce?

I planted the seed, Apollos watered it, but God made it grow. So neither he who plants nor he who waters is anything, but only God, who makes things grow. The man who plants and the man who waters have one purpose, and each will be rewarded according to his own labor.
I Corinthians 3:6-8

If God breaks the ground for you to plant a seed, He also has someone who will water it until the day of harvest for His glory. If you fail to plant the seed, there will be nothing to harvest later. Just as you are praying that someone will plant a seed into the heart of your prodigal spouse, you must use the opportunities that God creates for you to be a positive witness to others.

Although we have been discussing one-minute testimonies for marriage restoration, the Christian can have an arsenal of one-minute testimonies, ready to throw at anything Satan brings up, as God provides those brief windows. You can have a testimony of how you came to Christ and another of how God has met your financial needs. Your testimony of healing can be shared many times over.

Regardless of the topic, the God-given opportunity is not intended to share what you have done, nor what some ministry has done. God wants to hear you testify what He has done for you. What a mighty God we serve. May we always honor Him in our testimonies.

Now to him who is able to do immeasurably more than all we ask or imagine, according to his power that is at work within us, to him be glory in the church and in Christ Jesus throughout all generations, for ever and ever! Amen.
Ephesians 3:20

MONDAY MORNING QUARTERBACKS

The fear of the LORD is the beginning of wisdom; all who follow his precepts have good understanding. To him belongs eternal praise. **Psalm 111:10**

During football season every Monday, scores of men are replaying the weekend football games with one another. These chats always include someone's comments about what they would have done differently to bring about another outcome to the game. Talk around the coffee pot is often begun, "That coach should have. . ." or "He made a mistake by not. . ." It is easy to be a Monday morning quarterback, when the individual giving advice has nothing to lose if someone were to actually follow their advice with disastrous results.

Charlyne and I want to caution you about following the advice of Monday morning quarterbacks as you seek God's restoration of your marriage. Above all else, remember that God has spoken to y-o-u and given you His promise for your family. Why then, would you seek out and follow the counsel of other people, who have nothing to lose, when your Creator has already given you His perfect plan?

The people we seem to hear about most often attempting to be Monday morning quarterbacks for the marriage of someone else include:

1. Ministry telephone prayer partners - When you call, they hear the desperation in your voice. In a few seconds, they listen to your story and give you advice designed to temporarily relieve your pain. This often includes a suggestion to "get on with your life." What did God promise to you and not to them?

2. Family and friends - Like telephone prayer partners who do not know, the people who love you do not want to see you hurting, so they suggest a long term fix (with eternal consequences) for a temporary problem, just to dry your tears. What did God promise to you and not to them?

3. Pastors - A Barna Research survey revealed 47% of our senior pastors do not hold to a Biblical world view that encompasses the foundations of our Christian faith. If a man of God cannot agree with such basics as the virgin birth of Jesus and the presence of the devil, why should we expect them to pray for God working a miracle in your marriage? What did God promise to you and not to them?

4. Media ministers - The fact that an individual minister is on radio or television does not validate everything they say. I heard a radio pastor explain in detail how divorce is allowed by God for hardness of heart. He continued to explain how each of us have areas of hardness in our hearts, thus opening the door to divorce to almost anyone. What did God promise to you and not to them?

5. Counselors - If you are seeing a Christian counselor who prays with you and quotes Scripture as the source for their advice, you are fortunate. If your counselor is not praying with you and for you and your spouse, and is not opening the Bible, you are taking advice the world's way, regardless of what the sign on the front of the office reads. What did God promise to you and not to them?

6. Webmasters - The fact that a statement appears on a website does not mean it is true. For years, the medical community has cautioned against taking online medical advice, without checking elsewhere. It is time to use the same caution for marriage restoration. Any counsel from the Internet must be proven by you through Holy Scripture, otherwise you may be following bad advice, often from a stranger. What did God promise to you and not to them?

The bottom line, which you have heard from us time and again, is that if you are serious about marriage restoration, you must be listening to God and not to people. Your Lord

God loved you so much that He sent His only Son, Jesus, to die for your sins. God left the Holy Spirit here to lead, guide, and protect you, even through the valley of marriage problems you are in right now. Until some other individual can do that for you, listen to the One who did. What did God promise to you and not to them?

Everything you hear and every bit of advice you receive, must align with the Word of God. Do not accept someone's paraphrase of a verse of Scripture, nor the quoting of a partial verse, as a license for divorce or any other action. You must study the entire Scripture passage yourself, and seek out cross referenced Scriptures. By doing so, God will speak to you.

Charlyne and I are not exempt from our words being proven by Scripture. It is our prayer that everything we say or write will be checked by you against God's Word. By doing so, He can speak directly to you and to your situation. What did God promise to you and not to us?

You can find, with God's help, a pastor who preaches the Word of God and who believes every word of it is true. With God's help, discover a prayer partner who will stand with you for the restoration of your marriage, without offering their advice. Surround yourself with healthy, growing people, who can uphold you through the valleys without pointing out the way to the courthouse, and who can rejoice and praise God with you over His victories. Above all else, listen to God and not other sinful humans for your direction.

You must not listen to the words of that prophet or dreamer. The LORD your God is testing you to find out whether you love him with all your heart and with all your soul. It is the LORD your God you must follow, and him you must revere. Keep his commands and obey him; serve him and hold fast to him. **Deuteronomy 13:3-4**

WHAT HAVE YOU DONE WITH JESUS?

"For God so loved the world that he gave his one and only Son, that whoever believes in him shall not perish but have eternal life. For God did not send his Son into the world to condemn the world, but to save the world through him."
John 3:16-17

One evening, Charlyne and I stayed up until midnight watching television, something we seldom do. Earlier we had recorded a favorite program, "Pulpit Classics," which features videos of worship services from years past at Dr. Jerry Falwell's Thomas Road Baptist Church, in Lynchburg, VA.

The program that aired that evening was from a sermon preached over 30 years ago by Dr. J. Harold Smith. It was titled, "God's Three Deadlines." Dr. Smith gave illustration upon illustration of men and women who had missed one of God's three deadlines and God had called them into eternity. The night, when this sermon was preached at Thomas Road, over 2,000 people were saved in three great altar calls.

Dr. Smith spared no words in describing the Christless Hell, a place of eternal torment, for people who miss one of the three deadlines. They are the blasphemy of the Holy Spirit, sinning away your day of Grace, and sinning unto death.

We both went to bed with heavy hearts, thinking about the scores of prodigal spouses who are living so near to one of God's three deadlines.

Let's be clear that you are standing for your marriage for one main reason: so that your now-prodigal spouse will, by the grace of God, avoid the Hell where they are now headed. Marriage and full family restoration must be the result of the one you love coming to Christ.

I wish every stander could have sat in our family room late that Tuesday and heard Dr. Smith give examples of people who mocked God and were dead a few hours later. Without question, your view on standing for your marriage would have been different this morning. The things that seemed so important and so painful to you would pale compared to having your beloved go to Hell.

Here in the United States, our April 15 tax filing deadline is just over two weeks away. Many people are working feverishly to gather the information to complete their return. Each of us is looking for the bottom line of our tax return. The question is how will we end up?

The taxing situation of your marriage struggles also has a bottom line. That bottom line is a question: what have you done with Jesus? The answer could be multiple choice:

- You depend on Jesus for your every decision. As the old hymn says, "He walks with me and talks with me along life's narrow way."

- You acknowledge the power of Jesus, but do not have a personal relationship with Him. He is, in effect, your last resort in times of crisis.

- Jesus is known to you only as a good man or a historical figure.

- You are sensing the call of Jesus on your life and on your stand.

- You are asking, "Who is Jesus?"

That evening, it was nearing midnight when we saw Dr. Smith drawing the net, or extending an invitation to the people in that crowded church to confess their sins and enter into a personal relationship with Jesus Christ. He especially called for people with secret sin in their lives to respond. We watched as scores of people streamed to the altar of the church.

Many were responding from out of the choir. These people were not off the streets, but had been within the church for at least long enough to join the choir. I suspect that some sat through years of sermons, yet God chose that specific night, that time, to touch their hearts.

I wish it were possible to track each person who was in that church on a Sunday night 30 years ago. Some went on to mature and to grow in the Christian faith. There are probably men who are now pastors who were saved on that night. Others began the walk of a Christian, but somewhere fell away. A few might have stayed as no more than church members. I suspect there are people who, at that service, once more hardened their heart to the calling of the Holy Spirit. A few might have even missed one of God's three deadlines and are in Hell today.

"A farmer went out to sow his seed. As he was scattering the seed, some fell along the path; it was trampled on, and the birds of the air ate it up. Some fell on rock, and when it came up, the plants withered because they had no moisture. Other seed fell among thorns, which grew up with it and choked the plants. Still other seed fell on good soil. It came up and yielded a crop, a hundred times more than was sown." When he said this, he called out, "He who has ears to hear, let him hear." **Luke 8:5-8**

I wonder if there were standers or prodigal spouses in that great service. How fervently was someone praying for their prodigal to repent? Did they continue to pray until God touched their prodigal, or did they grow weary and give up?

The answer to your every question, to your every decision, to your every valley experience, is Jesus. He is waiting patiently to be your Friend, your Companion, your Comforter, and your Savior. Following Jesus is not one way to restore a marriage. It is the only way to restore a marriage. Anything else is a counterfeit.

Once you have reconciled your life with Jesus, Charlyne and I pray that you will continue to pray until every member of your family also knows Jesus personally. Your prayers and your stand can mean the difference between Heaven and Hell for someone you love.

What have you done with Jesus? If you are unsure, we invite you to visit the most important webpage on the Rejoice site - http://rejoiceministries.org/salvation.html

For the wages of sin is death, but the gift of God is eternal life in Christ Jesus our Lord. **Romans 6:23**

THE "D STRAIN" VIRUS IS SPREADING

Seldom does a day go by that we do not hear news reports about some kind of destruction or the devastation that a pandemic could do. There is another great threat, the D Strain, and it has already arrived.

This epidemic has already struck not only our nation, but simultaneously all around the world. Satan, the evil one is spreading this invisible, odorless, tasteless, mess over the people we love and care about, namely men and women who are standing with God for the restoration of their marriages.

Never before have we encountered so many standers who are on the verge of giving up praying and standing with God for (1) the salvation of a prodigal mate, and then (2) restoration of their marriage. The early effects of Satan's warfare are evident everywhere.

The evil one is attacking with the "D Strain" of sin which includes:

DOUBT – "Did God really tell me to stand, or was it something I dreamed up?"

DESPAIR – "This is hopeless."

DIVISION - Standers start majoring in the minor issues, instead of on the Word and Jesus. Soon their focus is on the issue, and not on their stand with God.

DEFEAT - If Satan can't defeat you, he will defeat someone whose defeat will defeat you. (This might be poor English, but good in thought.)

DISTRUST – "Can (or will) God really do what He has promised me?"

DISTRACTION - Looking at your own (or someone else's) circumstances instead of focusing on God.

DISPUTE - Attempting to fight the battles yourself, instead of allowing God to work.

DISENCHANTMENT – "My spouse is not changing so why should I try?" (Hey, what's happening on the other side of your mountain where you can't see?)

DECEIT – "No one knows about my secret sin." (But God knows and it is killing your stand for a healed marriage.)

DEVOURING – "I will write back and give them a piece of my mind!"

DEMANDS – "If God doesn't do something soon, I am giving up."

DATING – "This person is only a friend, and I am so lonesome. I can handle going out and still stand."

DIVORCE – "My divorce is final, so there is no hope for my marriage." Tony Evans once said, "It does not matter what the records down at city hall say. The records in Heaven say that you are married!"

The good news is that God has provided a vaccine to protect you against each and every element of the "D Strain." We beg you to please look up these verses, learn them, and memorize them. Post them on your mirror, so that when the enemy attacks your home, you will be protected by God's Word:

DOUBT – *"I tell you the truth, if anyone says to this mountain, 'Go, throw yourself into the sea,' and does not doubt in his heart but believes that what he says will happen, it will be done for him."* **Mark 11:23**

DESPAIR – . . .*and provide for those who grieve in Zion- to bestow on them a crown of beauty instead of ashes, the oil of gladness instead of mourning, and a garment of praise instead of despair. . .* **Isaiah 61:3**

DIVISION - . . .*so that there should be no division in the body, but that its parts should have equal concern for each other.* **1 Corinthians 12:25**

DEFEAT - *I can do everything through him who gives me strength.* **Philippians 4:13**

DISTRUST - *Trust in the Lord with all your heart and lean not on your own understanding; in all your ways acknowledge him, and he will make your paths straight.* **Proverbs 3:5-6**

DISTRACTION - *But Martha was distracted by all the preparations that had to be made. . . "Martha, Martha," the Lord answered, "you are worried and upset about many things, but only one thing is needed. Mary has chosen what is better, and it will not be taken away from her."* **Luke 10:40, 41-42**

DISPUTE - *Starting a quarrel is like breaching a dam; so drop the matter before a dispute breaks out.* **Proverbs 17:14**

DISCOURAGEMENT – *"Do not be afraid or discouraged because of this vast army. For the battle is not yours, but God's."* **2 Chronicles 20:15**

DECEIT - *Don't be deceived, my dear brothers. Every good and perfect gift is from above, coming down from the Father of the heavenly lights, who does not change like shifting shadows.* **James 1:16-17**

DEVOURING - *If you keep on biting and devouring each other, watch out or you will be destroyed by each other.* **Galatians 5:15**

DEMANDS - *Let us not become weary in doing good, for at the proper time we will reap a harvest if we do not give up.* **Galatians 6:9**

DATING – *". . . 'For this reason a man will leave his father and mother and be united to his wife, and the two will become one flesh.' So they are no longer two, but one. Therefore what God has joined together, let man not separate."* **Matthew 19:5-6**

DIVORCE - *Has not the Lord, made them one? In flesh and spirit they are his. And why one? Because he was seeking godly offspring. So guard yourself in your spirit, and do not break faith with the wife of your youth. "I hate divorce." says the Lord God of Israel. . .* **Malachi 2:15-16**

If you have decided to give up on standing, who will pray for your prodigal? Do you not care about their eternal destiny? What about the generational curse of divorce that is in your family that YOU have an opportunity to stop? Have you not grown strong enough in the Lord to withstand the attacks from Satan? They are predictable when you are doing Kingdom work.

This winter season there may be a shortage of flu vaccine, but our Lord God has vaccine available for you against the "D Strain." If you will allow God to vaccinate you today, you will be protected against the enemy's attacks tomorrow.

THE SUPER BOWL TICKET BOOTH

Everyone who competes in the games goes into strict training. They do it to get a crown that will not last; but we do it to get a crown that will last forever. 1 Corinthians 9:25

Two opposing forces are at work, not only in two football teams, but all across the land; not just on a Super Bowl Sunday, but every day of the year. They are the forces of light and darkness, of good and evil. Your marriage may appear to be many points behind, but today we want to tell you what the outcome could be if you allow our Lord Jesus to be Captain of your team.

FIRST AND TEN -

It seems that each Super Bowl Sunday, the entire world is ready to watch 22 men chase a piece of inflated pigskin up and down 100 yards. It is amazing how that can all be combined into many exciting scenarios.

Someone once said that football games are won or lost in the last two minutes. Your stand for a healed marriage will also be won or lost at the last minute. It will be lost only if you give up.

Super Bowl Sunday, as each touchdown is scored, we'll observe one team jumping wildly with excitement, while the other hangs their heads and frowns. At halftime in that game, the team that is losing will head for the locker rooms. It will not matter that the game is not over. The losing captain will declare, "I give up! This is hopeless. I just can't do this any longer. That other team will never change! I quit." Will this happen? Not hardly. Both teams will fight and give all they have right up until the last second, regardless of the score.

What are you doing when the enemy appears to be winning the battle for your family? Are you playing and praying even more intensely, or are you heading for the showers? We encourage you to stand firm with the Lord, following His leading, until your family is restored.

It is first and ten. Take that ball and score a touchdown for families.

I press on toward the goal to win the prize for which God has called me heavenward in Christ Jesus. **Philippians 3:14**

SCOUTING REPORT -

The stander's scouts are out and today we bring you their reports on two teams. Winning this game can be predicted, based on scouting reports. One group of standers is strong, both on offense and defense. They can not only take back ground by praying Scriptures and pleading the blood of Jesus over situations, but are also excellent on defense, praying a hedge of protection around their spouses.

Their play book is the Bible, and they only run plays that can be found there. That team's greatest asset might be their wireless communication system between the bench and their "Coach," who sits high up in heavenly places. He can see everything and always calls the right plays in any situation. Well maintained, this team's communication system never misses a call from above.

The other team's greatest weakness might be their communication system. It runs on the Internet, and frequently picks up plays, not from above, but from people in the stands. Everyone wants to help the Coach, feeling they know best. This team's time off the field is spent most often not in the practice of prayer, but at websites. Their play book is not the Bible, but some manual written by another player. Coaches never fumble, but there has never been a player who did not drop the ball once in a while.

The first team will come on the field prepared to fight until they receive victory. The second team is going to "try" this game. Some of those players will head for the locker room the first time they are tackled. Others will find excuse after excuse as to why they cannot continue to play. You may see them running to the sideline, asking the Coach, "How much longer do I have to do this?" "I am too tired to do this any longer." In fact, players on that second team may set their own time limits, while the first team is prepared to run, pass, play, and fight the opposition right up until the final buzzer sounds.

Based on our scouting reports, which team do you predict to win the Super Bowl of Marriage and to receive their rings?

You need to persevere so that when you have done the will of God, you will receive what he has promised. **Hebrews 10:36**

It's halftime. Visit our "concession stand" - http://stopdivorce.org

PERP WALK -

We have heard reports about scalpers selling Super Bowl tickets for greatly inflated prices, some in the thousands of dollars. The news also warns about counterfeit tickets that have been discovered. Each televised report usually shows what the media call the "perp walk," as the perpetrator is led off to jail with hands cuffed behind the back and a frown on the face and a stern faced police officer on either side.

We want to remind you that there are scalpers after your prodigal spouse. They have inflated the value of what has been promised to the one you love. Satan passed off a counterfeit as the real thing and the one you love is attempting to pay the price.

Although it may not be captured on film, there is coming the day of a "perp walk" out the front door of your home, as the enemy is bound and cast out, and your prodigal comes home. The enemy's sentence will be for life.

By the way, there will be one difference in your "perp walk." The bad guy will be escorted not by tough-looking police officers, but by our loving Lord Jesus Christ. He wants your marriage straightened out as much as you do. Continue to call on Him and trust Him for His help.

A WORD FROM CHARLYNE - THE GOAL:

*Brothers, I do not consider myself yet to have taken hold of it. But one thing I do: Forgetting what is behind and straining toward what is ahead, I press on toward the goal to win the prize for which God has called me heavenward in Christ Jesus. **Philippians 3:13-14***

Are you keeping your eyes on your goal of a restored marriage? I listen to the football players on television that are interviewed during the week, and regardless of the past week's scores and wins or losses, they are each saying that this is a new game and with new determination and hope that they are going to win the game regardless of who they are playing. Are you that confident today, in having your marriage restored? Why not? Our Lord Jesus Christ is your Coach. He knows all the plays that need to be made for your marriage to be restored and reach the goal that God has for you.

You must walk and run in confidence with your Lord Jesus Christ this Sunday. Sunday is such an important day for all Christians as we go and worship our Lord. We seek His face and His answers for all our problems. He is the

Way, the Truth and the Life. What a day for every Christian to pray for their lost loved ones, prodigal spouses and children to have their hearts touched by the Holy Spirit. They become like Saul into a Paul. Nothing is too hard for our Lord God!

Jesus answered, "I am the way and the truth and the life. No one comes to the Father except through me. If you really knew me, you would know my Father as well. From now on, you do know him and have seen him." **John 14:6-7**

Are you walking in despair and feel like you are on the losing team? Then you need to surrender your own will to the Lord first. Turn away from your own sins of unbelief, doubt and fear. Purify your heart, which will produce holiness and a Christ-like lifestyle. Halftime is over and now you need to give everything you have to following your Lord Jesus Christ to win this game and your restored marriage. Our Lord does not need a quitter, but one who will do everything to win this game.

Create in me a pure heart, O God, and renew a steadfast spirit within me. **Psalm 51:10**

I pray that as you watch football or any sport, you note the discipline and the endurance that the players have in giving all they have to win the game. We Christians often do not want to get dirty or fight the enemy. We want everything easy and given to us.

For everyone looks out for his own interests, not those of Jesus Christ. **Philippians 2:21**

Keep your eyes on the goal and listen to your Coach. He will get you the prize of having a restored marriage. Then you can give the praise to the Lord for He gets all the glory and honor in restoring every marriage. Let's give Him a big cheer today! We are on the winning team!

BUILDING CODES

He has caused his wonders to be remembered; the LORD is gracious and compassionate. He provides food for those who fear him; he remembers his covenant forever. **Psalm 111:4-5**

On some days, when I sit at my computer, I am looking outdoors on a grassy lawn and beautiful hedges. Today I am looking at a window about to be boarded up by a storm shutter. Intermittent rain squalls announce what is about to come our way. In the background the television is broadcasting warnings on how to prepare for the approach of Tropical Storm Katrina. It is expected to be a hurricane before it makes landfall and is presently sitting about 50 miles east of Fort Lauderdale, headed very slowly but very directly our way.

August is the anniversary of Hurricane Andrew which devastated many areas of South Florida. Even though years have passed, there are a few areas not yet reconstructed to pre-hurricane conditions. Full recovery is taking year upon year. Nevertheless, it is amazing to see what has been accomplished.

We also remember the anniversary year of divorce devastating the South Florida Steinkamp home. We are blessed by the Lord to be able to share our "before" and "after" stories with other men and women who are praying for the restoration of their families. Even though many years have passed, there are a few areas not yet reconstructed to pre-divorce conditions. Full recovery is taking year upon year. Nevertheless, it is a miracle to see what God has accomplished.

Why does the media go back and tell about old storms? Why do we go back and tell about old storms in our marriage? For the same reasons. Foremost, so that the rebuilt homes standing strong in 2005 will be storm-proof.

Many people are not aware that hurricane season is several months long. "Hurricane season" in a restored home, as well as in all marriages, is year round.

The same enemy that attacked your home in the first place can be relentless in his continued spiritual attacks after a prodigal spouse returns home. Satan wanted to destroy your home yesterday. His desire is to destroy it today, and he will aim to bring it down tomorrow as well. His attacks are on families who have the ability to accomplish much for the cause of Christ.

"Why bother ever attempting to rebuild a family?" you may be thinking. For the people of South Dade, they needed to have homes in which to live. The prodigal spouse you love needs a "spiritual home, for eternity." If you stop praying, your mate may die without Christ. The Bible also tells us that those who die without Him go to Hell.

"What about the comment above that some areas of your marriage are not yet reconstructed to pre-divorce conditions?" another might be wondering. The victims of Hurricane Andrew, as well as last year's four Florida hurricanes, returned home at the proper time. Then they began rebuilding.

A stander who feels that marriage restoration is complete when a prodigal spouse first comes home is akin to the victims of a hurricane propping up a few sheets of plywood on top of their demolished house and calling it home.

The homes being rebuilt in South Florida are under a new, stricter building code since Hurricane Andrew. It was discovered that many builders had become sloppy and had taken shortcuts. A home constructed today will be able to withstand the storms of tomorrow.

How is your home being reconstructed? By the world's standards or by God's? Are you proud of the solid construction, or are you cutting corners simply to get your "Certificate of Occupancy" as soon as possible?

Your prodigal spouse walking in the door is not the end. It is only the beginning of what God can do. The beautiful process of restoration will continue until the glorious day when the Lord calls one of you home to dwell with Him for eternity.

Your marriage is never going to be like it was before. The scar of separation or divorce will always be visible in your home, just as it is in ours. By Jewish traditions, scars are a reminder, not only of a previous injury but also of a deep wound that has healed well. Their purpose is said to be a reminder for us not to repeat the same mistakes again.

Our desire for your family is to see the present wound of marriage strife heal correctly. Left untreated or treated in the wrong ways, it will become infected and never heal. Remember, rebuilding and healing are both very slow processes. May both be done in God's time.

"Therefore everyone who hears these words of mine and puts them into practice is like a wise man who built his house on the rock. The rain came down, the streams rose, and the winds blew and beat against that house; yet it did not fall, because it had its foundation on the rock. But everyone who hears these words of mine and does not put them into practice is like a foolish man who built his house on sand. The rain came down, the streams rose, and the winds blew and beat against that house, and it fell with a great crash." **Matthew 7:24-27**

"Lord, help us all to rebuild our homes, not on the soft sand of what is worldly or popular, nor on the advice of man, but on none other than the Solid Rock of Jesus Christ. Amen."

WHAT DO YOU BELIEVE?

Therefore, since through God's mercy we have this ministry, we do not lose heart. Rather, we have renounced secret and shameful ways; we do not use deception, nor do we distort the word of God. On the contrary, by setting forth the truth plainly we commend ourselves to every man's conscience in the sight of God. **2 Corinthians 4:1-2**

What do you believe about your marriage restoration? If you are alone or at a place where you can say it out loud, say what you believe about your marriage. I wish we were all in an auditorium where we could hear each other declare, "I know God will heal my marriage," or some variation of that theme.

Why do you believe in your marriage being restored? Hopefully, you are not confident of marriage healing because the Steinkamps or anyone else has promised you. The only true answer is because God has promised that to you.

Before any church or organization ministers to your spirit, you should know what they believe about God, His Word, and the truths in the Bible. How do you know the people you are dealing with are in fact even Christians?

The people God sends to us come from a variety of spiritual backgrounds. Some were pastors or married to pastors. A large number are professing Christians, but not practicing Christians. (They did not live the Christian life.) For others, our teachings are the first time anyone has called for them to allow God to fill the God-shaped vacuum we each have deep inside our spirits. Regardless of their background, Charlyne and I strive to move every person entrusted to us to a closer personal relationship with God and His Son, Jesus Christ.

"What does this have to do with marriage restoration?" someone is asking. This IS marriage restoration. Without Jesus, my wife and I could give you no hope for your marriage. Granted, you may be able to manipulate your prodigal home for a season, but we want them home, heart and all, once and for all. That will happen when Jesus changes first you, and then the person you married.

I want to share the Statement of Faith of Rejoice Marriage Ministries. A word of explanation and supporting Scriptures has been added to each of the seven items:

REJOICE MARRIAGE MINISTRIES STATEMENT OF FAITH -

We believe the Bible to be the inspired, the only infallible authoritative Word of God.

In the beginning was the Word, and the Word was with God, and the Word was God. **John 1:1**

The law of the LORD is perfect, reviving the soul. The statutes of the LORD are trustworthy, making wise the simple. The precepts of the LORD are right, giving joy to the heart. The commands of the LORD are radiant, giving light to the eyes. The fear of the LORD is pure, enduring forever. The ordinances of the LORD are sure and altogether righteous. **Psalm 19:7-9**

. . . so is my word that goes out from my mouth: It will not return to me empty, but will accomplish what I desire and achieve the purpose for which I sent it. **Isaiah 55:11**

Charlyne teaches often that the Bible is the book for standers. Every answer you will ever seek is in the Bible. God can make it come alive to you in a way you may have never known before. Regardless of how many Harry Potter books have been sold, The Bible remains the most purchased book, year after year, because it is the Word of

God. You must settle in your own life, before anything else, that the Bible is God's Truth revealed.

We believe that there is one God, eternally existent in three persons: Father, Son, and Holy Spirit.

Then Jesus came to them and said, "All authority in heaven and on earth has been given to me. Therefore go and make disciples of all nations, baptizing them in the name of the Father and of the Son and of the Holy Spirit." **Matthew 28:18-19**

"All this I have spoken while still with you. But the Counselor, the Holy Spirit, whom the Father will send in my name, will teach you all things and will remind you of everything I have said to you." **John 14:25-26**

There is only one God, but He exists in three persons. Some religions worship other and many gods, but we worship the God who created all that is today. (A simple way to understand three in one is to look at water. It can be water, ice, or steam, but it is still H20.)

We believe in the Deity of our Lord Jesus Christ, in His virgin birth, in His sinless life, in His miracles, in His vicarious and atoning death through His shed blood, in His bodily resurrection, in His ascension to the right hand of the Father, and in His personal return in power and glory.

The virgin's name was Mary. The angel went to her and said, "Greetings, you who are highly favored! The Lord is with you." Mary was greatly troubled at his words and wondered what kind of greeting this might be. But the angel said to her, "Do not be afraid, Mary, you have found favor with God. You will be with child and give birth to a son, and you are to give him the name Jesus. He will be great and will be called the Son of the Most High. The Lord God will give him the throne of his father David, and *he will reign over the house of Jacob forever; his kingdom will never end." "How will this be," Mary asked the angel, "since I am a virgin?" The angel answered, "The Holy Spirit will come upon you, and the power of the Most High will overshadow you. So the holy one to be born will be called the Son of God." **Luke 1:27-35***

*For this very reason, Christ died and returned to life so that he might be the Lord of both the dead and the living. **Romans 14:9***

*After the Lord Jesus had spoken to them, he was taken up into heaven and he sat at the right hand of God. **Mark 16:19***

These are the basic truths of the Christian life. Had Jesus not come, we would be hopeless. He came, was crucified and died, was resurrected, and ascended to Heaven. But He left us with power over the enemy through the Holy Spirit. The Bible promises us that Jesus is coming again.

We believe that regeneration by the Holy Spirit is absolutely essential for the salvation of lost and sinful men.

*"For God so loved the world that he gave his one and only Son, that whoever believes in him shall not perish but have eternal life. For God did not send his Son into the world to condemn the world, but to save the world through him." **John 3:16-17***

*For the wages of sin is death, but the gift of God is eternal life in Christ Jesus our Lord. **Romans 6:23***

*Do not conform any longer to the pattern of this world, but be transformed by the renewing of your mind. Then you will be able to test and approve what God's will is - his good, pleasing and perfect will. **Romans 12:2***

*You were taught, with regard to your former way of life, to put off your old self, which is being corrupted by its deceitful desires; to be made new in the attitude of your minds; and to put on the new self, created to be like God in true righteousness and holiness. **Ephesians 4:22-24***

This is why you stand. Each of us needs to be saved from sin by realizing we have a sin problem that only Jesus can solve, then confessing our sins to God. Sin is not erased by good works, or by joining a specific church. Jesus died on the cross to pay the price for my sins and for yours.

> **We believe in the present ministry of the Holy Spirit, by whose indwelling the Christian is enabled to live the Godly life.**

*On one occasion, while he was eating with them, he gave them this command: "Do not leave Jerusalem, but wait for the gift my Father promised, which you have heard me speak about. For John baptized with water, but in a few days you will be baptized with the Holy Spirit." **Acts 1:4-5***

*"We are witnesses of these things, and so is the Holy Spirit, whom God has given to those who obey him." **Acts 5:32***

After Jesus was crucified for our sins, He arose. When God took His Son back to Heaven, He left us the Holy Spirit to "indwell," or live inside every one of us who turn to Him. The Holy Spirit is your constant companion today. The Holy Spirit will lead you, comfort you, and protect you, if you will make room for Him (by repenting of your sins) and then invite Him in.

> **We believe in the resurrection of both the saved and the lost - those who are saved to the resurrection of life, and those who are lost to the resurrection of condemnation.**

That if you confess with your mouth, "Jesus is Lord" and believe in your heart that God raised him from the dead, you will be saved. **Romans 10:9**

"I tell you the truth, whoever hears my word and believes him who sent me has eternal life and will not be condemned; he has crossed over from death to life. I tell you the truth, a time is coming and has now come when the dead will hear the voice of the Son of God and those who hear will live. For as the Father has life in himself, so he has granted the Son to have life in himself. And he has given him authority to judge because he is the Son of Man. Do not be amazed at this, for a time is coming when all who are in their graves will hear his voice and come out - those who have done good will rise to live." **John 5:24-29**

"Once again, the kingdom of heaven is like a net that was let down into the lake and caught all kinds of fish. When it was full, the fishermen pulled it up on the shore. Then they sat down and collected the good fish in baskets, but threw the bad away. This is how it will be at the end of the age. The angels will come and separate the wicked from the righteous and throw them into the fiery furnace, where there will be weeping and gnashing of teeth." **Matthew 13:47-50**

This explains why you are standing with God: to see your prodigal come out of sin and turn to Christ. We stand so our loved ones will gain eternal life.

> **We believe in the spiritual unity of believers in Christ. The evidence of that unity being shown by how we love one another.**

"A new command I give you: Love one another. As I have loved you, so you must love one another." **John 13:34**

Dear friends, let us love one another, for love comes from God. Everyone who loves has been born of God and knows

God. Whoever does not love does not know God, because God is love. This is how God showed his love among us: He sent his one and only Son into the world that we might live through him. This is love: not that we loved God, but that he loved us and sent his Son as an atoning sacrifice for our sins. Dear friends, since God so loved us, we also ought to love one another. No one has ever seen God; but if we love one another, God lives in us and his love is made complete in us. **I John 4:7-12**

True followers of our Lord Jesus Christ do not constantly fight and bicker with one another. We live in peace and harmony, following the example of Jesus when He walked on earth. If you, as a stander, are striving to represent Jesus to your prodigal spouse you must do so with unconditional love, overlooking faults, turning the other cheek, time and again, as the Lord has taught us.

The seven timeless truths outlined above comprise this Ministry's Statement of Faith. Everything we do is rooted in those truths. Some churches have a statement of faith that includes sub-points and doctrinal issues, but since this Ministry touches people from many denominations, we adhere to these basics of the Christian faith.

This message has a twofold purpose. First, Charlyne and I want you to understand what we believe. Secondly, even though we strongly encourage standers to be involved in a local church, the fact is that many are not. Because of this, we feel a responsibility to help them grow in the Christian faith. The very basis of faith is defined in a Statement Of Faith.

"Wow! Deep stuff," you may be thinking. While it may be deep, it is also wide enough to bridge the gap between Heaven and Hell for you, your spouse, and your children (see http://rejoiceministries.org/gulf.html). It is also wide enough to bridge the gap between the prodigal's pig pen and their family at home.

You have read what we, as a Ministry believe. Now I want to repeat the question that was asked at the start of this message, "What do you believe about your marriage restoration?" Today I encourage you to write out your own statement of faith.

Decide, based on Scriptures, what you believe and why you believe it. As the old country preacher said, "If you don't stand for something, you will fall for anything." Charlyne and I do not want that to happen to you. Marriages are restored for people who are fully trusting in God and living as He directs.

That is what I believe. What about you?

THE CHURCH CHOICE

"The Lord looked down from his sanctuary on high, from heaven he viewed the earth, to hear the groans of the prisoners and release those condemned to death." So the name of the Lord will be declared in Zion and his praise in Jerusalem when the peoples and the kingdoms assemble to worship the Lord. **Psalm 102:19-22**

Charlyne and I love our standers. In our book, men and women who have taken a stand with our Lord God, praying for the restoration of their marriage to a prodigal mate or for the salvation of a lost loved one, are among God's special people. In each day's *Charlyne Cares* we strive to follow the Holy Spirit's leading in bringing you something that will help you to stand. Many days, such as Saturdays when we send out testimonies, there is something to encourage you. On most days, Charlyne has spent hours in the Word of God to bring you instructions. There are other days when we feel led by God to address problems common to many standers.

It is a fact that many standers do not attend church. We want to explore the reasons why they do not and offer Scripture that might help you understand what God desires of you in this area.

On the day of Pentecost, when the Holy Spirit came, believers were meeting together.

When the day of Pentecost came, they were all together in one place. Suddenly a sound like the blowing of a violent wind came from heaven and filled the whole house where they were sitting. They saw what seemed to be tongues of fire that separated and came to rest on each of them. All of them were filled with the Holy Spirit and began to speak in other tongues as the Spirit enabled them. **Acts 2:1-4**

We can also read of the early church meeting together and of the results, to the glory of God.

Every day they continued to meet together in the temple courts. They broke bread in their homes and ate together with glad and sincere hearts, praising God and enjoying the favor of all the people. And the Lord added to their number daily those who were being saved. **Acts 2:46-47**

Many of the people the Lord allows us to get to know through Rejoice Marriage Ministries have accepted Christ and become Christians after their marriage crisis began. Let's look at a story from the early church of a meeting that lasted until midnight:

On the first day of the week we came together to break bread. Paul spoke to the people and, because he intended to leave the next day, kept on talking until midnight. There were many lamps in the upstairs room where we were meeting. Seated in a window was a young man named Eutychus, who was sinking into a deep sleep as Paul talked on and on. When he was sound asleep, he fell to the ground from the third story and was picked up dead. Paul went down, threw himself on the young man and put his arms around him. "Don't be alarmed," he said. "He's alive!" Then he went upstairs again and broke bread and ate. After talking until daylight, he left. The people took the young man home alive and were greatly comforted. **Acts 20:7-12**

"Greatly comforted!" Isn't that what you are seeking when your heart has been broken? From this example in Scripture, that happens in church.

Let's look at some of the reasons that standers do not attend church:

- "No one agrees with my stand. I get tired of going to church and being told to get on with my life, and that God has someone better."

What does the Bible say?

In the following directives I have no praise for you, for your meetings do more harm than good. In the first place, I hear that when you come together as a church, there are divisions among you, and to some extent I believe it. No doubt there have to be differences among you to show which of you have God's approval. **I Corinthians 11:17-19**

What do you suppose people said to Noah when He went to church? I doubt that a man who had heard from God that the earth was about to be destroyed because of sin would stay home on the Sabbath and drive nails. He would have been in the temple, praying for those who were lost. This man had heard from God and was building a boat in a land where it had never rained. Noah had to meet with God on the Sabbath to receive the strength to endure the ridicule and criticism for the next week.

What did Abraham hear at the assembly when he announced that God had told him to sacrifice his only son?

The bottom line is that these people of God had heard from God, just as you have, regarding the restoration of their marriage. The nay-sayers did not have the call. They could not be expected to understand Godly direction as a bystander, just as people do not understand why you cling to hope for a dead marriage.

- "It hurts too much to go to church alone."

There was a Sunday night just before Christmas 1985 when I had to leave church in tears. The children's choir, about the age of my own kids, was presenting a Christmas program. The front row was lined with proud parents with cameras. I thought about our three kids, in church with their mom about fifteen miles away. I thought how they would have no Dad with a camera at their program. I can recall standing alone in the church parking lot, with tears streaming down my face. I know now that was one of the many times when God was speaking to me to go home, just as He may be telling your spouse. Sooner or later, His voice becomes so loud and so frequent, if someone is praying for that to happen, that we prodigals have to obey.

Healing often involves hurting. We know standers who are today recovering from surgery. They are hurting, but they are also healing. Part of your healing may involve attending church alone, even when it hurts. Remember, you are not alone. The Holy Spirit is your constant companion.

- "My pastor says that I am in error."

It was he who gave some to be apostles, some to be prophets, some to be evangelists, and some to be pastors and teachers, to prepare God's people for works of service, so that the body of Christ may be built up until we all reach unity in the faith and in the knowledge of the Son of God and become mature, attaining to the whole measure of the fullness of Christ. Then we will no longer be infants, tossed back and forth by the waves, and blown here and there by every wind of teaching and by the cunning and craftiness of men in their deceitful scheming. Instead, speaking the truth in love, we will in all things grow up into him who is the Head, that is, Christ. From him the whole body, joined and held together by every supporting ligament, grows and builds itself up in love, as each part does its work.
Ephesians 4:11-16

From our experience, the pastor of the large church I attended, who knew both Charlyne and me, welcomed me and another woman in church together. During the same season, Charlyne was being called in and rebuked by her pastor, simply because she was following people of faith in refusing to give up on what God could do through my life. By the way, that same pastor remarried us suddenly.

After the Lord, your local church needs to be your number one source of support. To illustrate, your church is your stairway to a mature walk with Christ. This ministry, or any ministry, is only the handrail to assist you. You need to attend, to tithe, to serve and to pray for your local church, where you are being a lighthouse for marriage for many people to see.

If your pastor is practicing "heavy-handed shepherding," where your every step in the Christian faith is being dictated by a person and not by God, you need to ask God if you are in the right church. Do not allow the circumstances of confrontation to alter the conviction of your call from God.

- "I get as much out of television preachers as I do from going to church."

Charlyne and I have a Sunday morning favorite also. Each week, the program is automatically recorded and we watch a second worship service together. You should be praying for a Christian to befriend your prodigal mate. If the Holy Spirit sends your spouse to church this weekend and everyone is home watching the television, who would minister to your beloved? You need to be in church with your head high, asking God to allow you to be an example to everyone there.

- "My pastor is divorced and remarried, as is much of the leadership of our church. How can I expect them to support my stand?"

Divorce has been allowed to run rampant for the last few generations. It has now made its way from the pew to the pulpit. Let's allow the Word of God to speak for itself on qualifications for pastors and church leadership:

Here is a trustworthy saying: If anyone sets his heart on being an overseer, he desires a noble task. Now the overseer must be above reproach, the husband of but one wife, temperate, self-controlled, respectable, hospitable, able to teach, not given to drunkenness, not violent but gentle, not quarrelsome, not a lover of money. He must manage his own family well and see that his children obey him with proper respect. (If anyone does not know how to manage his own family, how can he take care of God's church?) He must not be a recent convert, or he may become conceited and fall under the same judgment as the devil. He must also have a good reputation with outsiders, so that he will not fall into disgrace and into the devil's trap. Deacons, likewise, are to be men worthy of respect, sincere, not indulging in much wine, and not pursuing dishonest gain. They must keep hold of the deep truths of the faith with a clear conscience. They must first be tested; and then if there is nothing against them, let them serve as deacons. In the same way, their wives are to be women worthy of respect, not malicious talkers but temperate and trustworthy in everything. A deacon must be the husband of but one wife and must manage his children and his household well. Those who have served well gain an excellent standing and great assurance in their faith in Christ Jesus. **I Timothy 3:1-13**

In recent times, pastors, evangelists and Christian musicians have been allowed to change wives and barely miss a Sunday on the platform. This is changing today, as national Christian publications have gone on record calling Christians to expect biblical standards for men and women of God. One of the reasons this is changing is because people like you do not give up, standing for God's work of a restored marriage as a witness to unbelieving people, both within the church and outside.

Should a divorced and remarried man be a pastor? We cannot say, but only let God's Word speak to the subject. If you are sitting under the teaching of a man of God who does not meet the requirements for their office, and your stand for marriage restoration is being strongly opposed, you need to seek God's will for your church home. Regardless, do not give up and stop going to church.

- "My unsaved husband is at home and I have been told not to go to church without him until he goes."

The enemy must be laughing at this thinking. God has your husband under your (and his) own roof, where you can pray for him, and live out by example all that the Lord has taught you– except that you don't go to church. You have been told about submission verses, such as:

Wives, submit to your husbands as to the Lord. For the husband is the head of the wife as Christ is the head of the church, his body, of which he is the Savior. **Ephesians 5:22-23**

God's will is never contrary to God's Word. We have established that God desires His people to assemble for worship. Nowhere in Holy Scripture are wives told to place a husband over God. Yes, the husband must not be overlooked for the sake of church and church activities, but each individual must find the mix that is God's will for them and not to say simply, "I don't go to church because my husband doesn't." You may go to one service a week, or attend at a time when your spouse is doing something else.

We have close friends where the wife attended church faithfully and the husband did not. During that time, one of their sons was saved. She has been a Sunday school teacher, carried kids to church and served in church leadership. Her husband attended only for special events, yet he welcomed his wife attending her church, and he is friends with the pastor. If she had followed the "stay-home-when-he-does" crowd, many people may not have come to know Christ, including her own husband. A few months ago my wife was honored to lead that husband to a personal relationship with Jesus, just days before that man died. He is in Heaven today because of the groundwork his godly wife put in place, attending church alone, year after year.

Wives, in the same way be submissive to your husbands so that, if any of them do not believe the word, they may be won over without words by the behavior of their wives, when they see the purity and reverence of your lives. **1 Peter 3:1-2**

Charlyne and I both know, from opposite views, how difficult it is to attend church alone. We also know how much comfort and encouragement can come from finding the place God wants you to serve and in filling the role that He has for you, regardless of your marriage problems. We pray that you will earnestly seek His will for you regarding faithful church attendance.

My soul finds rest in God alone; my salvation comes from him. He alone is my rock and my salvation; he is my fortress, I will never be shaken. **Psalm 62:1-2**

A LINE IN THE SAND

Let us discern for ourselves what is right; let us learn together what is good. **Job 34:4**

"I hate divorce," says the Lord God of Israel, "and I hate a man's covering himself with violence as well as with his garment," says the Lord Almighty. So guard yourself in your spirit, and do not break faith. **Malachi 2:16**

God often uses the most unlikely times to give us His message. One Friday evening, we had six of our grandchildren in and out of our home, centered around a school basketball game. We had taken four of them out to dinner and were to babysit the youngest. Sometime in mid-evening, Charlyne was chauffeuring kids, and I was home alone. I sat down to watch a minister on television speak about women who have had abortions and men who have forced women to kill unborn children. Suddenly God told me how to explain a long-term issue in marriage ministry: second marriages.

Please come with me as we eavesdrop on a pastor's office for three consecutive days. Each day that man of God has two different women come to him for counseling. On day one, the first woman who comes in is dealing with having had an abortion in the past. The second woman who comes for counseling is there because she had been through a divorce.

We could get hung up right here, sorting out whether the women were Christians at the time of these traumatic events in their lives, but what really matters is, (A) Does each woman have a personal relationship with Jesus Christ right now? And, (B) has she dealt with the event, be it abortion or divorce, as sin? The wise pastor would make it clear to the respective ladies that abortion is the taking of a human life, and also that God hates divorce. Above all else, the pastor would certainly remind both ladies how much God loves each of them, regardless of the sin in the past.

On the second day, two other women come separately to the pastor's study. The first is pregnant and has an appointment for an abortion. The second has a court date for divorce. Each woman is questioning if she would be in God's will to proceed with her plans. Would that man of God not caution each woman against going on with their planned actions? He would share Scriptures to demonstrate how much God values life, and also how much He values the family, an institution that He created. In dealing with the second two women, that pastor's goal would be to save both a life, as well as a marriage which affects many lives.

If you think our fictional pastor is having a taxing week, just wait until day three, and listen to the two women who come in for counseling. The first woman is deep in sexual sin. She reasons with the pastor, "If I get pregnant, I'll just have an abortion." The second woman is also in sin. She is married, but having an affair. Would not that pastor's goal be the same for both women: to have them come out of their sin before an abortion or a divorce is even an option?

Even though all six women came in with different circumstances, many of that pastor's concerns would have been the same for each one. Above all else, he would want to express to each woman that God loved them so much that He sent His only Son, Jesus, to die for people with sin problems, just like theirs. The pastor would make clear just how much God loves them, but also that He loves them too much to leave them in their current condition.

It is doubtful that our pastor would attempt to sort out for the abortive women, how many other children the man had fathered, nor who was a Christian at the time of conception. The two issues would remain that God loves sinners but hates our sin, and that there is a way out of their situation that will give glory to God.

For too long, ministers and ministries have attempted to draw a line in the sand over the divorce and second marriage issue. The problem is that each may draw the line at a different place, resulting in, not helping, but confusing sincere standers.

You, as a stander, need to draw your own line in the sand about divorce and second marriage issues, with God guiding the stick for you. This does not happen by reading a few isolated verses, nor by believing what someone else has told you, but only by your studying the appropriate Scriptures, in detail, even to the extent of cross referencing verses, and taking time to study sound commentaries.

"Doesn't the Bible address divorce and remarriage?" someone may ask. Yes it does, but even the scholars in Jesus' time could not agree on God's meaning of every inspired word dealing with divorce and remarriage. Jewish scholars from the first century have said it almost seems that God was leaving questions unanswered, knowing the sinful lives His people would live. If there is wiggle room in Holy Scripture that allows for divorce and remarriage, God's intent surely was forgiveness and restoration, not for the justification of sin.

There is too much work to be done for all ministries, in calling people to say no to divorce, and stand for the restoration of marriage. We do not have time to split hairs over the who, what, when and why of divorce. Charlyne and I view our calling as one of getting people with troubled marriages to Jesus. Once we do that, the Holy Spirit will fine-tune each individual's Christian walk. He, not us, will convict when the stander is in the wrong.

If you are a man or woman standing with God for the restoration of your marriage, your assignment is to stand strong, without wavering, and to be an example to people around you. Your calling is not to persuade others that you have all the answers on any issue, but to share with others that you serve a Lord God who does.

Charlyne and I hurt for people who have gone through either abortion or divorce. We know people who have experienced abortion in an effort to save a marriage. It is our prayer that you will not feel condemnation because of your past sin. Jesus came and died for you to be forgiven. Seek Him, not the words of people, to help you draw your personal line in the sand. Always strive to walk as far away from that line as possible.

If you have a divorce in your past, first deal with that issue as sin. Seek the forgiveness of God for your part in the divorce. After that, all the questions about what you should do will be answered by God when you draw close to Him. He has the perfect solution for your situation.

My message and my preaching were not with wise and persuasive words, but with a demonstration of the Spirit's power, so that your faith might not rest on men's wisdom, but on God's power. ***1 Corinthians 2:4-5***

STANDING BEFORE THE MIRROR

In the presence of God and of Christ Jesus, who will judge the living and the dead, and in view of his appearing and his kingdom, I give you this charge: Preach the Word; be prepared in season and out of season; correct, rebuke and encourage — with great patience and careful instruction. For the time will come when men will not put up with sound doctrine. Instead, to suit their own desires, they will gather around them a great number of teachers to say what their itching ears want to hear. **2 Timothy 4:1-3**

Early one Tuesday morning I stood before the mirror, ready to shave and to start my day. I had planned to spend most of the day sitting in front of a computer monitor, editing Charlyne's most recent audio Bible teaching. I did not plan to see even half a dozen people on Tuesday. My shaving was not as detailed as it might have been had my plans for the day been more involved.

Tuesday was also the day of the funeral service for a local deputy sheriff who had been slain while transporting a prisoner. Law enforcement officers from around the nation were in town to attend the huge funeral service at a Fort Lauderdale theater. Road closures had been announced because of the funeral procession, so I had arranged to put off ministry errands until another day.

South Florida was in an uproar over this senseless death. The elderly deputy was known for being personable and well liked, even by the prisoners he transported.

A few years ago when our grandson, Ryan, was three, he and I had a weekly tradition of breakfast at McDonald's. One morning as we were leaving, a Broward Sheriff's Office transport van pulled in and discreetly parked in the last space. My grandson was fascinated by the "bad boys truck" that he had seen on television.

The deputy exited the van and walked toward the restaurant. When he spotted my grandson staring at his van with big eyes, the deputy walked over to us and shook Ryan's hand. In less than 30 seconds, the deputy delivered a speech to Ryan that was part crime prevention and part Grandpa.

When a photo of the slain deputy was shown on television a few days ago, my now first-grade grandson exclaimed, *"That's my friend!"* Following the death, I wrote a letter to the editor of our paper describing the impact that deputy had on young Ryan.

After hitting the high spots of beard stubble, dressed in jeans and a plaid shirt, I sat down with a thermos of coffee to start my all-day editing project. At 11:30 A.M. the phone began to ring. *My letter to the editor had just been read at that well-televised funeral service, and my name given as the writer!*

By mid-afternoon, two television stations had tracked down the Steinkamp family and were seeking interviews about that chance meeting years prior that had prompted the letter to the editor.

That evening, exactly twelve hours after I had stood before the mirror, carelessly shaving because no one would see me that day, Ryan and I were standing before two television crews in our living room. I still wore the jeans and a plaid shirt from that morning, when I thought no one would see me all day. Before I went to bed Tuesday night, television viewers across South Florida had seen my face.

What do you suspect would have been my reaction, if while standing before the mirror that morning, the Holy Spirit would have cautioned me to shave carefully for the cameras? I would have laughed like Noah's friends, and those surrounding so many people in the Bible.

When and how will your prodigal spouse come home? Only the Lord knows that. We do know that it may be sudden. I discovered Tuesday just how suddenly things can happen. Time and again you have heard how suddenly prodigals come home. In some instances, it is so sudden that even we prodigals are not expecting it!

Tonight when you go to bed, please do so remembering your prodigal spouse could be repenting at that very hour. Tomorrow morning, when you stand before your mirror, not knowing what the day will bring, may you do so in confidence that God is moving on your behalf.

Remember, God does not announce endings; He only announces beginnings.

This message is being typed early Saturday evening. During this time of week, when non-Christian friends meet, one will often ask, "Do you have your lottery tickets?" Billboards across the state display the amount of the jackpot. At 11:00 P.M. tonight, winning numbers will be drawn, and there may (or may not) be one or two winners. (If you are standing with God, seeking marriage restoration and buying lottery tickets, something needs to change.)

There are many unanswered questions when looking in the mirror. One of the greatest is when our lives will end. Statistics say there are 15 people in our county who will not be alive 24 hours from now. There is a figure for your county as well. Standers are not immune to death, just as prodigals are not. Our assignment is to be prepared to meet our Lord God face-to face and for each of us to be prepared to live with Him for all eternity.

Death comes just as swiftly as did the events experienced last Tuesday. Instead of my day ending in the media, I could have ended in the morgue. Would I have been ready to meet Jesus? Will you be ready on that unexpected day?

That Tuesday was a wake-up call for me, to always expect the unexpected. The one event which is both unexpected, yet promised, is death. If you sense that you may not be ready to face God, Charlyne and I invite you to visit http://rejoiceministries.org/salvation.html for help with answering your questions about where you will spend eternity. We both encourage you to do that today.

For I am convinced that neither death nor life, neither angels nor demons, neither the present nor the future, nor any powers, neither height nor depth, nor anything else in all creation, will be able to separate us from the love of God that is in Christ Jesus our Lord. **Romans 8:38-39**

GETTING OVER THE OTHER PERSON

Finally, brothers, whatever is true, whatever is noble, whatever is right, whatever is pure, whatever is lovely, whatever is admirable—if anything is excellent or praiseworthy— think about such things. Whatever you have learned or received or heard from me, or seen in me—put it into practice. And the God of peace will be with you. **Philippians 4:8-9**

We received a panic email that was not unlike the wording of many we receive. Their spouse was on the way home right then, and they did not know what to do next. Charlyne and I share on this topic in books, in audio teachings, and in *Charlyne Cares*, but some people are so focused on their current problems they cannot prepare for restoration and are shocked when it happens. My goal today is to wake you up to one of the major stumbling blocks to the healthy restoration of a marriage relationship, after God brings the prodigal home.

How does a returned prodigal get over the other person? You, as a person standing with God for His restoration of your home, can make or break the restoration process, depending on how you deal with the other person issue.

The heart of the discerning acquires knowledge; the ears of the wise seek it out. **Proverbs 18:15**

Let's start with the facts. You may not like them, and you may not agree, but once you have walked the walk, with your spouse, away from the other person, your AMEN will come.

- Getting over the other person takes time. Your spouse must go through a grief process, measured not in days or weeks, but possibly one or two years. Yes, it is a grief process, just as if someone had died. Until you can allow your spouse to grieve the other relationship, you are not ready for restoration. Quite frankly, it will not work otherwise.

- Regardless of what they say, most prodigal spouses have another person. Please be prepared for the day when that is revealed to you.

- Your prodigal cannot tell the difference between love and lust.

- Most prodigal relationships become sexual at some point, regardless of what message is being passed back to home.

- Your prodigal does have feelings for the other person. After they come home, they will sense a tremendous obligation to the other person.

- The other person is there, even after your mate's homecoming. After restoration, you cannot stuff that individual in a closet and expect them to evaporate.

- The other person is a sinner for whom Jesus died. Are you praying for their salvation now? Will you personally continue to pray for their salvation after your prodigal spouse is home?

- Your returned prodigal will bring home reminders of that other relationship. I have written about how long I had a photo of the other woman behind the visor in my van. One day God told me that photo had to go.

- Your returned prodigal may attempt to justify their sin.

- Eventually, your returned prodigal will probably want to talk to someone about the other person. It may be a counselor or pastor, it could be you.

Someone is thinking, *"So why try?"* Because God has called you to stand, both before and after restoration. Both periods of time are the identical spiritual battle. If God has called you to it, He will provide the help from on high that you need.

Resist him, standing firm in the faith, because you know that your brothers throughout the world are undergoing the same kind of sufferings. And the God of all grace, who called you to his eternal glory in Christ, after you have suffered a little while, will himself restore you and make you strong, firm and steadfast. To him be the power for ever and ever. Amen. **I Peter 5:9-11**

The chain of events in too many marriages in which the spouse has come home is as follows: (1) God uses circumstances to drive (yes, drive) the prodigal home; (2) The stander adopts an *"I have arrived"* attitude and slacks off on praying protection on their returned spouse; (3) The front door of that home is then opened for Satan to come in once again; (4) The other person re-enters the picture; (5) The returned prodigal leaves for the far country-once again, leaving the stander asking, "What happened?" What happened is that the enemy, always on the prowl, discovered an entry, be it ever so small, and being intent on destroying your marriage, has attacked once again.

We have been remarried for over 20 years after our divorce, and neither Charlyne nor I feel that we have arrived. God's restoration is an ongoing process, even to this day. Neither of us feels we are immune from Satan's attacks. I may be a lot wiser, but I am as susceptible to Satan's attacks as I was on the day we remarried.

What does "*susceptible* to" mean? The dictionary gives the meaning as "*capable of.*" Do you get it? Since I am still capable of sin, Charlyne prays and fasts more today, for me, for all our family and for all standers, than she did when we remarried.

So what is the bottom line for getting over the other person? For the stander, it is to never stopping praying, put the Armor of God on your returned spouse, and on every family member. It will take time for your returned prodigal to get over that person. When I first returned, everything I saw, read, and did would remind me of the other woman. Gradually, with Charlyne's prayers and time, those intense grief emotions began to subside.

For the prodigal, it means **no contact with the person** you are attempting to get over. If there is a non-covenant child involved, ask God to show you how to work out no contact. You cannot visit where you used to live in sin, sitting around with the other person under the guise of visiting your non-covenant child. If you do, you are dropping a lighted match into a gas can that will explode the marriage you are attempting to rebuild.

By all means, the prodigal is responsible emotionally and spiritually as well as financially for any non-covenant child born to another person. He or she must support the child God allowed to be birthed.

My prodigal friend, if you will have no contact for six months, you may be over that other person and ready to love your spouse in a new way. This may mean finding a new way to work, or even finding new work, but it must be done.

To both stander and prodigal, if you are serious about getting over the other person, and not looking for loopholes, you each have two great allies. Foremost, is the Holy Spirit of God. If you are praying and asking God's help, He will make possible avenues that you and I can not even imagine. Your second ally is time. The returned prodigal's drumbeat can be, "With God's help, in every way and every day, I am getting better and better."

Speaking of loopholes, a non-covenant child must never become a loophole for spending time with the other person. We each know what activity brought about that birth, and so every prodigal with such a child must seek every alternative to contact with that other person, for the sake of your marriage.

Let's imagine I asked you to pick up an item from a person with a deadly infectious disease, a disease to which you were highly susceptible. Don't you think you would be working with everything you have on an alternative means of delivery?

The person with which you had a child has the disease of adultery, a spiritual disease to which you have already proven to be susceptible. We have known grandparents who relay non-covenant children for visitation. Possibly your pastor could help or have suggestions on how weekend transfers could be made. The spouse who prayed you home could even come to the point where they could transfer the child for your visitation. As an added bonus, that praying spouse could be silently praying for the other person, eye to eye, when that precious child is picked up.

The spiritual war for your marriage is a winnable war. One of the largest weapons the enemy uses to keep things disrupted is that third person. You and your spouse can have victory through our Lord Jesus Christ.

While I was preparing this message one Monday morning, my radio was on very low in the background. I heard a well-known national pastor relate a story of a woman he had counseled. She was living with a man who was not her husband. The woman knew what she should do, but told the pastor she just could not break off the living arrangement. This wise man of God had a solution. She was counseled to go to the courts and get an order for the man to leave. She did so.

It was December when I met the other person that I had to go through the grief of getting over after Charlyne and I remarried. It took longer to get over that other woman than the relationship had lasted. As with everything Charlyne and I do, we want to help others avoid the pitfalls that attempted to ensnare our marriage.

BLUE

"He performs wonders that cannot be fathomed, miracles that cannot be counted." **Job 9:10**

You may have wondered how Charlyne and I can demonstrate such zeal for marriage restoration, year after year. Yes, God healed our marriage, even after a divorce. How can we be certain that He will do the same for you? A small piece of label maker tape, with the word **BLUE** on it caught my attention again recently. It may help explain why my wife and I are certain that we serve a miracle-working God.

Like most of us, my morning routine is identical every day. Tuesday, while opening the medicine cabinet in our bathroom, I noticed the **BLUE** label inside the cabinet door. I confess to being guilty of forgetting where God has brought me from, until I saw that label.

In 1993, while in Tulsa to speak at a marriage conference, I suffered my first stroke. God healed me. Charlyne and I were on a plane home within five days. During testing, a brain tumor was discovered in my brain.

In 1995 I suffered a more serious stroke that left me totally paralyzed. Within a few weeks, I progressed from bed to a walker to a cane, praise be to God.

Two years later, after speaking at a marriage conference in New York, I again became ill and was diagnosed with bleeding in my brain. Following surgery, I started to have seizures and suffered another stroke. I was in ICU and Charlyne was told that I might not survive. The Lord told her differently, just as He told her about our marriage. After weeks in ICU, an episode with blood clots that could have been fatal, and a serious fall from a wheelchair, God once again answered a wife's prayers. I was once again wheeled into a rehab unit and walked out weeks later, praise His name.

Then they cried to the LORD in their trouble, and he saved them from their distress. He sent forth his word and healed them; he rescued them from the grave. Let them give thanks to the LORD for his unfailing love and his wonderful deeds for men. **Psalm 107:19-21**

As a result of the damage, I had memory problems. The **BLUE** sticker that I noticed was placed inside that cabinet door when I could not remember the color of my toothbrush. It was **BLUE**. Instead of asking Charlyne, *"Which toothbrush is mine?"* two or three times a day, I could open the cabinet door and be reminded.

My **BLUE** sticker days seem far removed, yet they seem like only yesterday. Along the way, there have been two heart attacks and other health issues. My Lord Jesus has brought me through each and every one, praise God, even when the doctors told Charlyne, "This could be it. There is too much wrong."

Isn't that what people are telling you right now? *"There is too much wrong. Your marriage is dying."* What does God say? His Word is all that matters, so why do you even listen to others? I can type these words to you today because I have a wife who learned how to pray, to really pray, while I was a prodigal. Her prayers have saved my life, time and time again.

Do you have any miracle reminder stickers in your life? While mine says **BLUE**, yours may say **JOB**, or **FINANCES**, or **KIDS**. What has God done for you that was nothing short of a miracle? If your answer is, "Nothing," I pray the Holy Spirit will help you to recall miracle upon miracle that has happened to you. Why should you stop short of expecting another miracle-the restoration of your marriage?

Don't be deceived, my dear brothers. Every good and perfect gift is from above, coming down from the Father of the heavenly lights, who does not change like shifting shadows. James 1:16-17

My **BLUE** sticker reminds me of something else. Had my wife stopped praying and interceding for me to come back to Christ and to a praying family, and had she not prayed me through illness upon illness, there would be no **BLUE** sticker today. My wife could be **BLUE** because I died and entered eternity without Christ.

My toothbrush handle has changed colors many times since those **BLUE** days. Nevertheless, the sticker remains intact. It is my reminder of what God can do when people pray.

Have you suffered so much for nothing - if it really was for nothing? Does God give you his Spirit and work miracles among you because you observe the law, or because you believe what you heard? Galatians 3:4-5

AVOIDING BLOWOUTS

Let us fix our eyes on Jesus, the author and perfecter of our faith, who for the joy set before him endured the cross, scorning its shame, and sat down at the right hand of the throne of God. Consider him who endured such opposition from sinful men, so that you will not grow weary and lose heart. **Hebrews 12:2-3**

It will be like saying good-bye to a friend. The big silver van that Charlyne and I have traveled in for ten years has to go. The custom made matching trailer will also be going. Four-dollar-a-gallon gasoline being burned by a V-10 engine in a one-ton van does not compute. Soon someone else will be taking highway naps on my bus interior that I had built. I wonder what the new owner will be storing in those cabinets that we had made to store our books.

I quite literally traded down. I went from climbing up into the van to slinking down behind the wheel in the four door sedan replacement. I never knew a vehicle seat could rest so close to the road.

Last Thursday I took my replacement car to the garage we have used for years. Deep inside, I was secretly hoping a problem would be found, large enough for Charlyne to say, "Let's just keep your van."

Instead the service manager only shared those three dreaded words, "You need tires." When he explained that we "should" be able to get a few thousand more miles out of the old ones without any problem, I envisioned sitting alongside an interstate highway, cars whizzing by, while Charlyne and I waited for someone to change the tire.

While I waited for new tires to be mounted, I thought sitting by the roadside was not the worst thing that could happen. A front tire could have blown out, causing us to leave the road or roll over. Either or both of us could be killed, because I pushed the old tires beyond the limit.

It breaks our hearts that Christian men and women are having spiritual blowouts every day, simply because they neglected the things on which their journey with Jesus Christ rides.

Far too often our nation is abuzz with the news that another church or political leader has suffered a spiritual blowout, disabling him by the road of life. Please allow me to remind you that your soul is just as valuable to God as is that big wheel's, pardon the pun. God does not want either of you to have a spiritual blowout.

The world we are now living in has values all confused. A leader falls and the media interviews everyone who ever knew that person. We have yet to hear the first stern face anchorperson reporting, "Jill Smith, a stander, went out on a date with another man Saturday night and did not come home until Sunday morning. We have reporters looking for answers, but we are able to confirm that Jill did not attend church on Sunday. Stay tuned here for breaking news on this story of another fallen stander."

Even though it is not reported, we can assure you that standers have spiritual blowouts much more often than politicians and preachers. Anyone who falls into sin breaks the heart of God.

"It's different, because they are so important," you might be thinking. How do you know what God has planned for you and your spouse five years or fifty years from now? You might become the parents of someone like Billy Graham or Fanny Crosby, the author of thousands of the hymns we sing. It might be the will of God to give you a future pulpit to the world, if you can avoid spiritual blowouts. In addition, your circle of influence today is certain to extend far beyond what you can see. People are

watching to see how you handle your marriage crisis. Please do not disappoint them by having a spiritual blowout.

How can spiritual blowouts be avoided? Just as I did with the tires, on my newer smaller car, maintenance is needed before a blowout takes place.

Tire experts tell us that to keep our tires in the best possible condition, we need to keep them inflated to the proper pressure. Over time tires tend to lose a small amount of air. The same can be said of the Christian life. A one-time salvation experience, in which you confessed your sins and asked Jesus to forgive them, will not maintain your spiritual walk.

We need to consider church worship as the time when we allow God to put His pressure gauge on us, as we hear biblical preaching and apply it to our lives to determine how we are measuring up. If not done, someone will be going spiritually flat or suffering a spiritual blowout.

The garage where our auto work is done will check tire pressure any time a customer stops by. If a tire is low, they will air it up. Sadly, few customers take advantage of the offer until they have a flat. It is also sad that not all Christians show up to have God check their spiritual tires.

Just as a garage uses a hose to get tires inflated correctly, God uses our prayer time (time spent in His presence) and time spent in the Bible to keep our spiritual walk inflated.

I suspect that every parent, grandparent, aunt or uncle has had the experience of attempting to blow up a child's ball or toy by mouth. It looks so easy, but we can blow until the face turns purple and we are out of breath, and little progress has been made. A trip to an air pump blows up the toy in a few seconds. Time spent in God's presence is like a trip to His spiritual air pump.

Good tires also require proper balance. If not, the vehicle can shudder and shake. Likewise, every Christian (and every stander) also needs to be properly balanced. We have known standers to become so fixated on one issue that they ignore the rest of their spiritual journey. Sadly, some men and women allow their stand for marriage restoration to become their focus. They keep their eyes on their spouse and not on Jesus. All the talk is about what their spouse has done, not about what Jesus is doing.

Good alignment is also critical to maintaining good tires. Have you ever followed a car that was so far out of alignment that it almost seemed to be going down the road sideways? In living the Christian life successfully, it is important that we each personally be aligned with the Word of God, living every moment by God's direction. Alignment also helps to avoid spiritual blowouts.

When tires are purchased, the store might offer a road hazard warranty. In the event you damage a tire because of some obstacle you struck, the warranty will replace the tire. God also offers us a warranty against damage to our soul, caused by sin. Regardless of what you have done during your marriage or during your stand, when you confess and repent He is ready to forgive you.

. . .for all have sinned and fall short of the glory of God, and are justified freely by His grace through the redemption that came by Christ Jesus. **Romans 3:23–24**

If we go on a 2,000-mile trip and everything is fine until we have a blowout a mile from home, our tires failed us. Our goal was to finish well by arriving home safely.

Many religious leaders, and many standers, have run the spiritual race with excellence, but they had a blowout before arriving at their eternal home, Heaven. If Jill had been standing for Jack for ten years and then had a blowout, God's will is not accomplished in that marriage.

We know of many men and women who ran well, but allowed the enemy to come in by some small way, causing a blowout before they reached home. A race not finished well has not been run.

There's one more thing about tires. Unless you are riding a unicycle, tires function in multiples. I could have bought one tire, but left the other three in danger of a blowout. That would not have helped much. Nevertheless, there are people who attempt to walk through the Christian life alone. They are not active in a church, nor do they have a personal prayer partner in whom they can confide; someone who will agree with them for the Lord to meet their needs. These Lone Ranger Christians are setting themselves up for a spiritual blowout.

Leaders who are headed for spiritual blowouts are the first to know of their own approaching problems. They do not suddenly wake up one day and say, "Good morning, Lord. I think I will sin today." Satan has planted a seed of sin in their unprotected head. Given time, that seed will be fertilized by a lack of attention to the things of God. It will go from head to heart to hand, where they act upon it and have a spiritual blowout.

Standers who are destined for spiritual blowouts also are the first to recognize what is happening. They become too busy for time alone with God. Hours at the computer or on the phone chatting with others become their spiritual time. Their values start to slide ever so slightly. Maybe coffee with the opposite sex isn't so bad, or the wedding band comes off. They go from reading the Bible to reading worldly magazines with no thought. Secular television replaces the praise music that once filled their home. Left unchecked, casual dating with a male friend starts. Eventually, thoughts of their stand are only a memory. Their former spouse, for whom they once prayed so fervently, can literally go to Hell.

We praise God that He is the AAA service for spiritual blowouts. Regardless of how spiritually disabled you may feel today, once you call on Him and repent, (change your ways), He will soon have you traveling the Christian highway, the road to restoration, once again.

Our goal is to see you traveling the highway of life, arm in arm with Jesus, moving every day toward a marriage restored by Him. It must be healed in His way and in His time so that it will last. Charlyne and I are thankful that He has called us to help you keep your spiritual tires in good shape, so that you will see victory, not end up in a ditch with a spiritual blowout.

For the LORD gives wisdom, and from his mouth come knowledge and understanding. He holds victory in store for the upright, he is a shield to those whose walk is blameless, for he guards the course of the just and protects the way of his faithful ones. **Proverbs 2:6-8**

WE NEED HELP NOW!

So, if you think you are standing firm, be careful that you don't fall! No temptation has seized you except what is common to man. And God is faithful; he will not let you be tempted beyond what you can bear. But when you are tempted, he will also provide a way out so that you can stand up under it. **1 Corinthians 10:12-13**

Do you remember the television commercial for a home monitoring device to summon help in the event of a fall? In the ad, an elderly woman had fallen. She summoned help by pressing a button on the pendant she wore around her neck. In seconds, she was surrounded by paramedics, family, and neighbors. Our family knows from experience those devices do work. We had one for my dad during his declining years.

Right up front I confess this message comes from personal experience. One of my strokes resulted in an ankle that turns in from time to time, causing me to fall. I have fallen at home. I have fallen in New York's Times Square. I have fallen in Penn Station. I have fallen in the post office. I have fallen in hotel lobbies in Nashville and Virginia Beach. I have fallen so many times that my doctor tells me the cane is mandatory, before I suffer a major fall injury.

There is nothing more humiliating than lying face down in a public area and having people running to help. The noise my large frame makes hitting the floor brings more help than any button I could have pushed. One thing is for certain when I fall. If Charlyne is anywhere around, she will be the first person at my side, coordinating efforts to get me up and checking for injuries.

On the Saturday before Memorial Day I fell while putting up our flag, so I was going slow and hurting before this next incident. Ryan, our seven-year-old grandson was at our home for a weekend sleep-over. He also had an issue to

147

discuss with me. Ryan wanted to know why his sister and his cousins were on *Stop Divorce Radio,* but he was not. Ryan volunteered that he had memorized Psalm 23 and could recite that for the radio.

What Grandpa could refuse a request like that the night before Father's Day? Soon Ryan and I were headed for the small sound room we have at home so he could recite Psalm 23 for the radio. Ryan was standing between the chair and the counter, ready to become a recording artist. As I entered the door, I forgot that our scales were there. I went flying, pinning Ryan between the chair, the control board and the wall. I ended up on the floor smothering my little buddy.

"Grandma," came the feeble cry from underneath the overturned chair. "Come quick. We need help now!" I was fearful that my little buddy had been crushed like a bug. Once again, Charlyne responded instantly and sorted everything out. Thankfully Ryan was not injured. Later he joked that if we had a video of what happened, we could make a lot of money.

May I ask you a question? When the prodigal for whom you are praying is sent home by God, how many times will you allow them to fall?

A dozen years ago, following my discharge from rehab after one of my strokes, Charlyne was working all day and then caring for me at night. Whenever I needed to go down the hall during the night, I would have to awaken Charlyne. She would turn on her light, get up, position my walker, and then stand by while I slowly moved ten feet down the hallway. After the return trip, she would tuck me in bed, turn out her light, and fall asleep again, only to have me awaken her again, for the same reason, in a few hours.

During the wee hours of one of those early days, I decided that I was well enough to make that trip alone. Charlyne was exhausted, so accidentally awakening her would not be a problem. I managed to sit on the edge of the bed, get my balance (as best I could) lean out and reach my walker. Slowly I stood up and began to move, making my way all the way to my destination. When I started back to bed, I lost my balance, and ended up waking Charlyne by calling out to her from the bathroom floor.

What if she saw me lying there, headed for the phone, called the Rehab Unit, and asked, "What is going on here? He came home, but fell again. He's on the bathroom floor. No one told me that it would be this way. I thought he was healed. If this is the way that it's going to be with him getting up, only to fall again, I don't want him. You can have him."

That wasn't exactly her response. First, she made sure I was not injured. She offered to call 911 or our sons, but together we decided how I could get up. Charlyne prayed and I managed to scoot myself into the hallway. She positioned a chair in front of me. After 45 minutes I was back in bed. The only damage was a bruised ego.

What will be your response when you wake up to find your returned prodigal on the floor once again? I can assure you that it is very difficult to learn to walk again, both after a stroke and after a separation. Even with God's help, in our humanness the victims of both stumble around a bit. Even if we do stumble, we are still home. Your response to a stumbling spouse must be the same as Charlyne's response when she found me on the floor at 2:00 A.M. She prayed for me. A comment that, "You will never change" would only delight the enemy trying to destroy your family.

What will your reaction be if the one you love comes home, and then falls again?

Our example is found in Jesus Christ. How many times have you or I "fallen" from what God wants? How many times has He picked us up, dusted us off, and pointed us in the right direction once again?

Your returned prodigal will need to grow strong in the spiritual incubator of God's love and forgiveness right in your home. That will not happen when you, as a stander, start complaining and making threats every time your beloved stumbles. This is not a license to sin, but will allow your mate the opportunity to grow strong in the Lord, right under your prayers of protection.

May I ask you a second question? Have you, as a stander, fallen and can't get up? Are you tempted to give up because you can't get up? Regardless of what you have done, regardless of the mistakes you have made, Jesus is standing there today, saying, "Let's get you up. You can make it." On this day may you allow Jesus to get you "standing" once again.

You have a prodigal spouse, who needs your prayers. I am praying that you will make today a new day in your quest to handle your marriage problems God's way.

I know from being there, it is a long way up from the floor of the pig pen of life. It doesn't seem as far when we can see our covenant spouse and Jesus, standing there to help us up, once we prodigals reach out to them.

*But as for me, I watch in hope for the Lord, I wait for God my Savior; my God will hear me. Do not gloat over me, my enemy! Though I have fallen, I will rise. Though I sit in darkness, the LORD will be my light. Because I have sinned against him, I will bear the Lord's wrath, until he pleads my case and establishes my right. He will bring me out into the light; I will see his righteousness. **Micah 7:7-9**

IN TIMES LIKE THESE

"Does God listen to his cry when distress comes upon him? Will he find delight in the Almighty? Will he call upon God at all times? I will teach you about the power of God; the ways of the Almighty I will not conceal." **Job 27:9-11**

What a day we are living in! Gas prices go up, while the value of the dollar goes down. Unemployment, health care and the housing crisis are acknowledged by politicians. Each claim to have a solution, yet doing right versus doing wrong often escapes our elected officials. Often they cannot even agree on right and wrong.

On top of it all, you are in a marriage crisis.

An old hymn reminds us that:

"In times like these you need a Savior, In times like these you need an anchor; Be very sure, be very sure Your anchor holds and grips the Solid Rock!

This Rock is Jesus, yes He's the One; This Rock is Jesus, the only One! Be very sure, be very sure Your anchor holds and grips the Solid Rock!"

Fort Lauderdale, the large city near us, has as its nickname, "The Venice of America." This title can be rightly claimed because at one time, in my lifetime, Fort Lauderdale had more miles of canals than paved streets. Each year, The City of Fort Lauderdale and our city, Pompano Beach have a Christmas boat parade, with dozens of decorated water craft. Boat dealers are everywhere.

One of the restaurants where we take visiting standers is situated on the Intercoastal Waterway, the main canal in

South Florida. It is an interesting experience to sit during the winter months, in short sleeves, with a stander from the frozen north, in an outside dining area and watch million-dollar yachts leisurely make their way by on the Intercoastal Waterway.

When any of those yachts have problems, the first thing they do is to drop anchor. If they had an emergency and do not drop anchor, the yacht would soon be driven into a seawall or bridge by the currents. Once the anchor is dropped, the yacht is safe. The problem can be addressed before it becomes an emergency.

When marriage problems temporarily disable a family, the first step should be for one spouse to drop anchor. If not, the currents of public opinion from family, friends, counselors, and churches, could soon drive that person into something that might damage and sink their marriage once and for all.

The initial stage of marriage problems is a desperate stage. We know, because Charlyne and I lived through those days many times during our first 19 years of marriage. Each time, we would keep bailing water on our own and put another temporary patch on our ship of marriage. That would hold until we hit another hidden hazard on the sea of matrimony. Not until after we sank in divorce court, did Charlyne "drop anchor" and start, with the help of God, to do her part in starting to overhaul the boat of our marriage.

Men and women who are facing a marriage emergency are, at first, desperate people. They attempt to stabilize the marriage by dropping anchor anywhere they can. Some drop anchor in the opinions of friends. Others drop anchor in divorce and start over with someone new. People will drop anchor anywhere help is promised them, without regard to the validity of the source. Others even pay excessive charges to be allowed to drop anchor in some program, promising to heal their marriage. Sooner or later, each of these anchors will tear loose and the individual, once again, finds himself adrift.

Our sons have both had boats. It is a fact of life that boating is often as much about keeping the boat running as it is about actually having the boat move along the water. Nevertheless, neither son has ever decided to sink his boat because the motors were sputtering. Yes, the repairs may be costly and inconvenient, but the boat is worth keeping. Why then, do people decide to jump overboard from their marriage because of temporary problems?

If you are attempting to maneuver today in a marriage that is in trouble, the first thing you must do is to drop anchor. Protect yourself and your family from future damage until you, your spouse, and your marriage can be tuned up by the Manufacturer, our Lord God.

If you are sputtering along today, not knowing if you will make shore, you need to anchor in the Rock, our Lord Jesus Christ. As the Bible tells us, He is ". . .*an anchor for the soul, firm and secure.*" Place your trust in Him alone today. Stop looking at and listening to others, but allow Jesus to be your Navigator through this storm.

Our community has something else that many areas do not. We have several tow services for stranded boats. They seek out stranded boats and tow them to a dock or repair shop, for a hefty fee. In one incident, two competing tow boat operators ended up in a fist fight on the deck of a luxury yacht, stranded in the ocean off our coast. After the Coast Guard arrived, one man was arrested and the other ended up towing the disabled yacht.

If your marriage has become disabled, two opposing forces are vying to help you. Satan, the enemy of your soul, wants to steer you into the generational curse of divorce, possibly causing generations of your family yet unborn to not enjoy all they are created to be, to have and to enjoy. People may miss Heaven as a result of the effects of your divorce. On the opposite side, the Holy Spirit, through whom God reveals Himself to us, is inviting you to allow Jesus to take over what is not working in your life and family today. In the Bible, the book of Ephesians tells about this unseen spiritual battle.

May this be the day that you decide to drop anchor, once and for all, on the Rock of Ages, our Jesus.

We have this hope as an anchor for the soul, firm and secure. It enters the inner sanctuary behind the curtain, where Jesus, who went before us, has entered on our behalf. He has become a high priest forever, in the order of Melchizedek. **Hebrews 6:19-20**

UNDERGROUND

The man from whom the demons had gone out begged to go with him, but Jesus sent him away, saying, "Return home and tell how much God has done for you." So the man went away and told all over town how much Jesus had done for him. **Luke 8:38-39**

A few days ago I read an article about the underground church that was an eye-opener. Many of us, starting with yours truly, take our religious freedom for granted. We can decide when and where we will worship. We can decide what Bible we will read and when we will do our reading. It is up to us individually if we want to place symbols of faith on our vehicles, our home, and our clothing. We can worship and pray without fear of reprisal.

It is frightening to read of the extremes people in some parts of the world must go to for self-preservation when they assemble with other believers. May God forgive us for taking our religious freedoms so lightly.

A few years ago I spoke with a doctor from Russia whose family had just come to the United States. I asked him what aspect of American life amazed him the most. He replied it was the many choices in the grocery store. His life had been spent in an area where there was one product of each type, and items were often not available. His wife was having difficulty learning how to buy groceries in our stores, with all the choices.

Can you imagine the reaction of someone from the underground church when first introduced to open Christianity the way that you and I know our faith? If given the choice, no one would want to return to the underground church.

Do you know there is one aspect of Christian life in the free world that a few people prefer to keep underground by choice? A small number of men and women who are praying for marriage restoration and trusting God for His results want to keep it a secret from their family, their spouse, and their circle of friends.

Being an underground stander raises two questions:

- **If your prodigal spouse does not know you are standing, how will they know they are forgiven and welcomed back at home?**

- **If the people around you do not know you are standing, how much glory will God receive after He performs the miracle of marriage restoration? Your testimony will be diluted to people who do not know what you are praying for.**

One night the Lord spoke to Paul in a vision: "Do not be afraid; keep on speaking, do not be silent. For I am with you, and no one is going to attack and harm you, because I have many people in this city." Acts 18:9-10

My wife came out of an underground stand over 20 years ago with her spiritual guns blazing and has never looked back at being a silent and secret stander. If you have ever been in a restaurant with Charlyne you know what I mean. Her brown Bible will be open on the table, and it does not matter who overhears when she is talking about her Lord and marriages. Even the unexpected presence of a server at the table has no bearing on the length of her prayer.

When we were divorced, Charlyne told me she was standing. Even greater, she demonstrated to me that she was standing. Some people seem to have a misconception of what this is all about, so let me tell you what my wife did. Above all else, she did not beat me over the head with her faith or her stand. She did make me curious about the changes I witnessed in her life.

There came a point when the Lord directed Charlyne to call me and ask for forgiveness for her part in our marriage failing. During that same call, she briefly explained her stand and added something like, "I'll be sitting at home waiting for you until I'm eighty and in a rocking chair, but if you wait until then, you'll miss the best part!" If you have never been there, you cannot imagine what comfort that brings to a confused prodigal spouse, knowing the person you once married, but are now futilely attempting to forget, is not going to ever forget you.

How did Charlyne demonstrate her stand? Above all else, I could no longer push her buttons. The things that used to send her up a wall now seemed not to touch her. It was as if the emotional keyboard on which I once typed strife-causing statements had suddenly locked up. Regardless of what I did, and trust me I tried, she would not react in the wrong way.

Any request I made of Charlyne was granted with a smile. *"You want to change visitation days? Sure, no problem. Could I bring them to you?" "The check will be late? I understand." "Do not even be concerned about what you said to me. I know you were stressed. You're forgiven." "You want the family pictures? I know you could use them, so let's divide them up and you take whatever you want."*

Even in matters involving the other woman, my "ex-wife's" feathers could not be ruffled after she surrendered her life and marriage to the Lord Jesus. She then allowed the Holy Spirit to direct her life, so it was not necessary to seek man's opinion for her decisions.

Charlyne did not beg, but her Spirit-led actions were always right on time. The birthday card with, "PS-I'm praying for you," would arrive on a difficult day. The little "Love ya" written discreetly in my wife's handwriting and sent with some forwarded mail always did something inside me. I began to wonder about this woman who was losing weight, and now always smiled, but never seemed to get upset. Did I ask her to stop? No prodigal is going to ask their spouse to stop something they enjoy. Unfortunately, some overzealous standers who cross the line to begging and harassing, cause problems.

My wife remains the greatest stander I know. She did not start that way, but allowed the Holy Spirit to perfect her, to fine-tune her, until this prodigal husband discovered in her all that I was seeking in a wife. I know my wife, and her heart for standers. Her greatest desire is to have you to become just like Jesus. How? By turning to the Lord. Become like Jesus, not Charlyne, and follow only His directions.

Our Ministry goal is for every person who turns to us for help to mature in their personal relationship with the Lord Jesus. We want to see you carry out God's revealed will for your specific circumstances, just as He has directed you. For eighteen years, Charlyne has taught standers "Don't take polls." Now we add to that statement, ". . . and don't listen to opinions from people." You need to listen to God for your every decision.

Should you tell your spouse about your stand? I do not know, nor does any other human, but God does. Ask Him for the right answer. Be available to Him, and He will direct you.

People are praying around the world that the underground church will be able to come out into the open, to the glory of God. My wife and I are praying that every underground stander will also come out in the open, also to the glory of God.

"'Call to me and I will answer you and tell you great and unsearchable things you do not know.'" **Jeremiah 33:3**

FALSE STARTS

Then Jesus told them this parable: "Suppose one of you has a hundred sheep and loses one of them. Does he not leave the ninety-nine in the open country and go after the lost sheep until he finds it? And when he finds it, he joyfully puts it on his shoulders and goes home. Then he calls his friends and neighbors together and says, 'Rejoice with me; I have found my lost sheep.' I tell you that in the same way there will be more rejoicing in heaven over one sinner who repents than over ninety-nine righteous persons who do not need to repent." Luke 15:3-7

From my personal experience and from ministry experience, I suspect that most prodigals who have returned home and stayed home to see their marriage restored, have done so after a few false starts. The pull toward home by the Holy Spirit is so strong, but then the enemy tugs us back in the opposite direction.

For the sake of illustration, at times, it is much like two boys playing tug of war on the playground. Just when one appears to be winning, the second gives a tremendous tug on the rope that once again brings things back like they were, but please do not think that God is in a battle of power with Satan. It is your spouse on one end of the rope, and the enemy on the other. Your marriage is in the center for the winner to claim.

We were divorced. I had been offered a job out of town. I had quit my job locally and given notice that I was breaking the lease on my efficiency apartment. Suddenly the out-of-town offer was in question. I was to be told in a few days if the offer was still open. I faced being unemployed, with no place to live. My first thought when I hung up that doubtful phone call was, "If this all falls through, I will move home."

Why did I consider going home? Because my wife had told me that the door at home was always open for me, regardless of the circumstances and at any time. I called her and explained my dilemma, but even before calling, I was confident of what her reply would be. She had told me, not only in words, but in her actions. Does your prodigal know they are welcome back?

Our prodigal men and women are going to Hell, living in sin and running from Christ, while some make a game of standing with God and praying for their mate's salvation.

The Lord sends prodigals home to standing spouses who are praying to Him, and who are ready to welcome a hurting, wounded prodigal home, in any condition and under any circumstances.

...to open their eyes and turn them from darkness to light, and from the power of Satan to God, so that they may receive forgiveness of sins and a place among those who are sanctified by faith in me. **Acts 26:18**

The false start toward home will come for your spouse. When it does, you must always be prepared to intensify your praying, your spiritual warfare, your time with the Lord, and your stand with Him.

It is mandatory that during false starts you deal with any hatred or bitterness toward your spouse. As my wife says so wisely, you need to "*zip the lips.*"

In my false start, the enemy pulled his end of the rope, and the job came through. The other person was off to help me move. Did Charlyne give up over all this? You know the rest of the story. I can assure you that after that incident, when I knew I was welcomed at home, I began to have false starts in rapid-fire succession, until the day I obeyed what the Holy Spirit had been telling me to do for two years.

160

Your spouse can be manipulated back home, but that is not God's plan. If you do, this is not a false start; it is a stall. You know what happens to airplanes that stall--they crash. The Lord wants to change you first, and then your mate, rebuilding your marriage on the solid rock of Jesus Christ.

If your prodigal is making false starts toward home, and then backing out or disappearing, stand strong and rejoice because God is at work in the life of your resistant mate.

Search me, O God, and know my heart; test me and know my anxious thoughts. See if there is any offensive way in me, and lead me in the way everlasting. **Psalm 139:23-24**

THE LETTER FROM A PRODIGAL SPOUSE

Honey,

How in the world did I wind up out here? I just wanted to have some innocent fun and things just got out of hand. It took more and more fun to keep me happy, until the guilt was more than I could handle. So I left. Maybe I was not as mad as you thought, but I just knew that I did not deserve to be married to you. I thought once I was away from you that the guilt would go away, but it hasn't. I only feel more guilt about leaving. The world says divorce is OK and that I am on my way to becoming a "swinging single," but so far it looks like I am on the way to being a sad single.

Not to cry, but things are rough for me also right now. Do you think it is pleasant to be uprooted from your entire life and replanted in a land where guilt, sin and shame prevail? It is not. I know, it was my decision, but I had to do it. Besides, it was almost as if it really wasn't me doing those things. I wish I did not even know the word "divorce."

I do not mean those things I say, such as, "I never loved you." We both know that is just not true, but saying a lot of stuff is just part of this whole mess. You are not a bad person. In fact, you are a pretty neat person. That must be why I think about you about a hundred times a day (but have never told anyone that part before). I am trying so hard to look happy, but am slowly dying on the inside.

"Then why don't you come home?" you must be wondering. I just can't, even though I think about that often. What would others think? Besides, I do not know how to break it off with you-know-who. They do not know that I am even writing you. If I came home, I would have a hard, hard time putting all this behind me. Would you be patient enough to let me heal? It will (I mean it would, sorry) take time and a lot of work from both of us. Did I tell you I dreamed about you and I praying together? It was only a dream.

The best I have ever felt in a long time is when I heard that you were praying for me. My prayers right now only go as high as the ceiling. So I do not pray, but I know God is still there. He did not go away just because I turned my back on Him, but I was ashamed to really seek Him after all that I did. I know that God would never allow me in Heaven now, so thanks for your prayers that are keeping me alive on this earth.

What does "standing" mean? You need to get on with your life. I stopped believing in fairy tales a long time ago. I am never going to come home, but would like for us to be friends. I will call you to talk about our being friends-just friends. No, I can't because you-know-who forbids me to call. I do not know why there is such a strange pull on my life from that corner.

I could come over and talk to you. That would feel good. I need to lie to get out, so that would make you like the other person, so I can't do that either. I feel like a caged animal most of the time. Would you want me home just as I am, confused and all? Probably not, after all that I have done to us.

I think this needs to be delivered in person, maybe left at your (our) door. I will bring my things with me, just in case I happen to see you and you say yes to my coming home. I can get out of this other mess later, if you are willing.

Know what? My heart beats fast and I feel lighter when I plan how I could come home. It is like the weight is off me. This may be another of many false starts, but I am practicing coming home today. Sure hope you are ready to receive me, warts and all.

From someone who really never stopped loving you.

GO HOME!

*Here is a trustworthy saying: If anyone sets his heart on being an overseer, he desires a noble task. Now the overseer must be above reproach, the husband of but one wife, temperate, self-controlled, respectable, hospitable, able to teach, not given to drunkenness, not violent but gentle, not quarrelsome, not a lover of money. He must manage his own family well and see that his children obey him with proper respect. (If anyone does not know how to manage his own family, how can he take care of God's church?) He must not be a recent convert, or he may become conceited and fall under the same judgment as the devil. He must also have a good reputation with outsiders, so that he will not fall into disgrace and into the devil's trap. **I Timothy 3:1-7***

If America were ever to fall, the predicted progression is first individuals fall, then marriages fall, then churches fall. After all this happens, society, as we know it today, is ready to fall. Where are we right now? Without question, people have fallen. Look around at all that is happening, too much evil to illustrate. Consider the news reports you have heard in the past week.

As you know, marriages have fallen. So many people do not seem to care. Is the church in America strong enough to hold back the tide of Satanic attack that has already taken out individuals and marriages? Spiritual attack is at the church door, and in some instances, has already been allowed inside.

Each week Rejoice Marriage Ministries has contact with dozens upon dozens of hurting men and women from all across the land. Based on what we are hearing, in general the church in North America is unhealthy. In church after church, the men of God have become lukewarm shepherds.

How I praise God for churches where the pastor is a sold-out blood-bought servant of our Almighty God, striving above all else to win people to Jesus Christ and to mature them as Christians. His motives are not nickels and noses, nor notches in his pastoral belt, but the saving of souls, regardless of the personal cost. All across America, revival is taking place at churches pastored by shepherds like this. Sadly, those churches seem to be in the minority.

The pastor's study has become a death chamber for marriages, as men and women with broken hearts over marriage problems hear not the promises of God, read from His Word, but the counsel to, "Divorce because you have grounds," and "God doesn't want you to be unhappy." Some are even hearing, "God has someone better for you." Why are wounded mates and their prodigals not told about the Cross of Calvary? The abandoned spouse is directed not to an altar, but to an attorney. Even though only separated, they are pointed toward divorce recovery classes, often the first step in finding a new mate.

The motto of many churches in dealing with a fractured marriage has shifted from "Hang on and let God work," to "Get mad, get over it, and get on with your life."

How we rejoice when we hear about a pastor who has taken on a prodigal church member who walked away from family and faith, praying and praying, and praying some more; loving the unlovable, until that marriage is healed. We are thrilled when we hear of a pastor going the extra mile to show a confused, sin-filled prodigal they are still loved, both by that pastor and by their God.

Why are pastors such a concern to me? Over twenty years ago, when we were divorced, I went to talk to one pastor. He did not know Charlyne, but handed me the book she was praying I would somehow receive. I did not like what that pastor said, nor what the book said, **(Go home!)**, so I went to see a second pastor, different church, miles away.

He listened to my plight, and then read Scripture to me to bring home his point: **"Go home."** On that July day we suddenly remarried, I drove south with the words from the book ringing in one ear, and the counsel from the second pastor ringing in the other. The message was the same: **"Go home!"**

How often from the pulpit at your church do you hear, "marriage restoration," or "marriage put back together again," or "marriage restored," or "marriage healed," or anything along that line? Just consider what would happen if every pastor in the world was praying for marriage restoration every week! That is where we need to be. If we are praying for the sick, why not the sick marriages?

There may come a day when your prodigal spouse somehow sits down in a pastor's office. I pray they will be dealt with as straightforward as I was; not looking for loopholes, but a man of God sharing what the Bible says about marriage, divorce, and the family. Your prodigal needs to be directed home, not into another relationship. We need to pray there are pastors like that across the land.

It is not too late to stop the slide to destruction of individuals, families, churches, and then society. The horse is out of the individual's gate, as well as the family's gate. It is at the church's gate. Let's pray that our pastors turn to God 100% and recognize what is happening before it is too late.

*But just as he who called you is holy, so be holy in all you do; for it is written: "Be holy, because I am holy." **I Peter 1:15-16***

ROAD HAZARDS

So, if you think you are standing firm, be careful that you don't fall! No temptation has seized you except what is common to man. And God is faithful; he will not let you be tempted beyond what you can bear. But when you are tempted, he will also provide a way out so that you can stand up under it. **1 Corinthians 10:12-13**

One Friday I traveled across Alligator Alley to pick up an order of books that had been reprinted in Naples, Florida. While on the straight, flat road that cuts through the Florida Everglades, I spotted something in the road far ahead. I slowed down and pulled to the right, and the driver beside me pulled to the left, leaving a huge truck tire casing between us.

I was not so fortunate several years ago while traveling through Atlanta at rush hour. The same type of tire casing flew off a truck directly in front of me. I could not swerve and it was too close to stop. My only option was to drive over the huge black item. It damaged both the van and our trailer.

Today I feel led to warn you about debris that may be lying on your road to marriage restoration. If you strike it, your stand could be damaged or even ended. It is my goal to make you aware of the obstacle, so that like me on Alligator Alley, you can carefully avoid hitting the debris.

Satan is the driver of the truck ahead of you on your road to restoration. He causes road debris to fall into your path and delights when a stander hits something that hinders what God is doing in the life of both you and your spouse. The evil one's primary road obstacle is the opposite sex.

During these years, Charlyne and I have known scores of serious standers who have hit restoration road debris. Here are some of the most common areas:

- Renewing friendships with an old opposite sex friend.
- Phone calls with someone calling, "just to see how you are doing."
- Justifying a relationship with the opposite sex as "just friends."
- Feeling an email relationship is harmless due to the miles between.
- Saying or thinking, "I can handle it" regarding any relationship.
- Telling your details to the spouse of a friend.
- Becoming involved in a singles ministry. (You are married!)
- Being one-on-one with someone of the opposite sex.
- Playing around with online dating services.
- Failing to have advance standards for dealing with the opposite sex.
- Fantasies about what kind of husband or wife someone would make.
- Slacking off on personal devotions, prayer time, and Bible reading.
- Seeing how close to the line you can live, instead of how far from it you can stay.

Are my wife and I being old fashioned? Not really, because we know how subtle Satan can be and how much he wants to stop your journey to marriage restoration. In addition, you are hurting and vulnerable during this time. Any attention or affection from the opposite sex, regardless of how innocent it is intended to be, sets off all kinds of thoughts and emotions in your mind.

May I make application? Jill is a stander. Her best friend sends her own husband by to handle a home repair for Jill. After he finishes, Jill gives the friend's husband a hug. To Jill it means thank you, but to the man it could mean, "That divorcee is climbing all over me." That night, Jill, lying in bed alone, wonders what kind of husband the man might be. In a couple days, the man decides to stop by Jill's to see how the repair is holding up. Jill is flattered by the male attention. This time, the exit hug is a bit longer and then, BAM! Another stand just hit debris on the road to restoration.

Jack, a male stander, attends a church where people hold hands for prayer. One week, he sits beside an attractive woman. During prayer, while holding hands, Jack thinks he senses the woman giving his hand an extra squeeze. The next week, Jack positions himself in the seat next to the woman. After church he starts a conversation. All that week, Jack had been thinking. . . BAM!

The items listed above are not copied from a romance novel, nor are they something Charlyne and I have dreamed up. Each has happened to multiple standers just like you, men and women who wanted so very badly for God to save their spouse and to heal their marriage, but who hit something in the road that sidelined them.

What got me started on all this? Our recent ministry tour was eye-opening. Charlyne and I met scores of solid standers, striving to always do things God's way. We also witnessed situations and heard comments where standers are leaving themselves wide open to the enemy's subtle attack in this area.

When Charlyne was standing, and I was out prodigalizing, my wife was always so cautious to avoid situations or relationships that could turn wrong, not only because of what I might think, but also because of what others might think.

God has called us to stand with you and encourage you, but also to warn you about perils along the road to restoration. Just like my book run on Friday, we want to see you arrive back home safely, and not hear that you are sidelined in the Atlanta of adultery by something Satan placed in your path.

But my eyes are fixed on you, O Sovereign LORD; in you I take refuge—do not give me over to death. Keep me from the snares they have laid for me, from the traps set by evildoers. Let the wicked fall into their own nets, while I pass by in safety. **Psalm 141:8-10**

HOW MUCH DO YOU TRUST GOD?

"O Sovereign LORD, you are God! Your words are trustworthy, and you have promised these good things to your servant. Now be pleased to bless the house of your servant, that it may continue forever in your sight; for you, O Sovereign LORD, have spoken, and with your blessing the house of your servant will be blessed forever."
2 Samuel 7:28-29

Early one morning my wife and I were doing devotions together, a blessing in itself. Charlyne wanted to read a verse in another translation so she picked up my burgundy Bible, sat back down, and started turning to a specific verse.

I do not think I really heard the verse Charlyne was reading. Observing that particular Bible opened and lying in my wife's lap, I had an overwhelming thought: twenty-something years ago I never would have envisioned Charlyne ever touching my Bible again, much less having her reading it to me.

When I moved out of our home prior to the divorce, that Bible is the one I took with me. Sadly, for over two years it was only a window dressing to me. Most Sundays I could be found in church carrying that Bible. It went right along with the wing-tipped shoes and the dark suits in impressing women other than my wife. In fact, I wore out the Bible's cover, not by use, but by carrying it in and out of church as well as to some places where neither that Bible nor I should have been.

We had that Bible re-covered a few years ago, and every page inside was carefully retained by the bindery in the restored Bible. Today it still has page after page of notes I took during sermons with women other than Charlyne sitting beside me. After all, taking notes went right along with the impression I was attempting to create, but inside I was as hollow as could be. Some of the notes are so pointed, clearly telling me to go home, that now I read them and wonder how I could have been so dense.

Frequently we hear from people who are praying for their marriage and whose prodigal spouse has started attending church with the other person. Most express, in one way or another, "My spouse could not attend with me but now they have the nerve to attend with someone else. How could they?"

If your prodigal is attending church, regardless of the reason, you should be thanking God. It is never a bad thing for a person to be hearing the Word of God proclaimed in their presence, regardless of what motivated them to attend church. If your prodigal is living in sin, you should especially be thanking God that He has the one you love in church. Our Lord God is right there with that odd couple.

There are incidents in the Steinkamp story that have never been told, out of respect for the other people involved. I do feel led to share that many Sunday afternoons after coming back from church, the other woman and I had serious discussions about something from the sermon dealing with adultery. I never would have admitted it then, but both of us were under Holy Spirit conviction.

I need to ask you a very serious question; **how much do you trust God?** Please ponder it and not just give the standard answer about how trusting you are.

*Blessed is the man who makes the LORD his trust, who does not look to the proud, to those who turn aside to false gods. Many, O LORD my God, are the wonders you have done. The things you planned for us no one can recount to you; were I to speak and tell of them, they would be too many to declare. **Psalm 40:4-5***

On the day you were saved you trusted God. On the day when you took a stand for marriage restoration you trusted God. Do you still trust God that much today?

When God sent your prodigal spouse to church with another did He not know what He was doing? Did God slip up when He allowed your mate's non-covenant marriage to that other person to proceed, despite your prayers? When that other person became pregnant by your spouse, God's Word tells us He was right there.

*For you created my inmost being; you knit me together in my mother's womb. I praise you because I am fearfully and wonderfully made; your works are wonderful, I know that full well. **Psalm 139:13-14***

There have been many incidents in our own family when we have wanted to question what God was doing. Where was God when our grandson was stillborn? What about the times in our family when we prayed for healing and it has not come? Where was God when five male family members were out of work because of a business failure? *(If you feel that families in ministry have it made, you are headed the wrong direction. Serving the Lord full time is like waving a red flag at a bull. Satan will pull out all the stops to bring down people in ministry.)*

I pray that you will join Charlyne and me in realizing that God is right there with each of His children, regardless of what they are passing through.

*God is our refuge and strength, an ever-present help in trouble. Therefore we will not fear, though the earth give way and the mountains fall into the heart of the sea, though its waters roar and foam and the mountains quake with their surging. Selah. **Psalm 46:1-3***

Someone might be saying, "I would never have let that Bible back into our home because I know where it has been and I know who read from it with my spouse." It is not about who read from that Bible, nor is it about who sat in church with your spouse. It is about what God tells us inside every Bible.

"Every word of God is flawless; he is a shield to those who take refuge in him." **Proverbs 30:5**

Before we remarried, Charlyne allowed Jesus to vaccinate her with the lifetime vaccines of forgiveness and trust. Regardless of what she might face on this day, the matters of her trusting God and forgiving me are settled. My burgundy Bible is no longer a symbol of a hurting time for her, nor of a sinful time for me. For many years that sacred book has been a symbol to each of us of what God can do in the midst of that hurt and sin.

Regardless of what news about your prodigal spouse you might hear today or even if this season of no contact continues, rejoice and thank God that He is at work on the other side of the mountain. My prodigal Bible tells me so.

May the God of hope fill you with all joy and peace as you trust in him, so that you may overflow with hope by the power of the Holy Spirit. **Romans 15:13**

POWERFUL SHOVES AND GENTLE NUDGES

Although the Lord gives you the bread of adversity and the water of affliction, your teachers will be hidden no more; with your own eyes you will see them. Whether you turn to the right or to the left, your ears will hear a voice behind you, saying, "This is the way; walk in it." **Isaiah 30:20-21**

Many of the email and letters we receive and read each day follow the same format. First, a hurting and wounded spouse relates historical details of their marriage. Second, they outline what is happening right now. Third, they are looking for answers to hard questions they are facing. These life-changing decisions will impact the future of not only that person, but also the future, and possibly the eternal destiny, of their spouse, their children, and other family members. These are not matters to be taken lightly. They may involve legal concerns, financial matters, or child custody issues. Answers do not come easily.

There is often a fourth part to the correspondence we read. The stander, seeking help, often adds, "My friends say. . .;" "Everyone thinks I should. . .;" "My counselor told me to. . .;" "Everyone is telling me. . .;" "My parents said. . ." It is totally understandable how a man or woman facing these life changing, (and life-shattering) decisions would want to make certain they are 100% on target.

We rejoice when the writer of an email or letter reports distinctly, "I sense God wants me to. . ." or "I have prayed about this and God is leading me to. . ." Charlyne and I know this is a person whose marriage restoration vision is right on target.

If a rocket were launched to the moon, and it left Cape Kennedy only 1/10 of a degree off course, it would miss the moon by tens of thousands of miles. Can you see how the decisions you are making today, if they are not what God wants, could miss the mark of His will for your family by a long shot?

While preparing this message for you, I was watching a Monday convocation from Liberty University. The speaker was a returned astronaut, who is a Christian. The man shared video he had taken during his space trip. The most amazing image I saw was of the astronaut standing on the runway, in front of the returned shuttle. He explained the goal is to have the craft stop as close as possible to the center line. In his video, the center wheel was about two inches off the line.

Can you imagine! That shuttle had traveled into outer space and then landed only two inches from the bull's eye. If a man-made craft can be made to do that, can you and I not discover and walk in God's will every day?

We often reply to our correspondence by asking, "What is God telling you to do?" Many times the stander will then relate how they are having difficulty hearing from God. Often they are looking for God to give them a powerful shove in the right direction, when that is not His way. Our Lord leads and guides each of us with His gentle nudges.

Do you recall the video of an assassination attempt on President Ronald Reagan as he was entering his limo outside a Washington hotel? A Secret Service agent saw what was about to happen, and in a split second floored the President, attempting to knock him out of harm's way. That is how we often expect God to guide us in making decisions. The Holy Spirit gives gentle nudges to each of us, in the way we should go and the actions we should or should not take.

I can tell you in all honesty that God speaks to me all day long. Hopefully, I am listening and obedient. He is not shoving me around, but gently guiding me. Obedience is my part of His speaking to me.

Early this morning, I was sharing with Charlyne about a meaningful devotional that I had just read. She had a Scripture that amplified the subject we were discussing. God was speaking an affirmation to her, through His Word, of a task that He has for her to do. At the same time, I sensed that the Lord would have me to share in *Charlyne Cares* today. I am writing, and Charlyne is in her office working on a different project. God did not need to knock me off my feet, President Reagan style, in front of the keyboard to reveal His will to me and to my wife.

The issue is not if an individual is receiving messages from the Lord, but if they are hearing Him. If your television was turned on, but with the volume all the way down, would that set still be receiving sound? Certainly it would, but you would not be listening. We each need to be careful that we have His Holy "volume" turned up to a level where we can hear.

What are some of the major distractions to a person hearing from God?

Busyness - God speaks to us in every imaginable situation. Returned prodigals share interesting stories of where they were and what they were doing when they finally listened to the Lord's voice. We each still hear from God best when the distractions are minimized. In the evening, put aside the magazine and newspaper and spend time in His presence. Walk away from the computer, and instead of being interested in what people are saying, develop a hunger for what God is saying to you. (God speaking to you personally-what an awesome thought!) On the way to work, turn off the CD and listen to God's plans for you for that day.

Tiredness - It is more difficult to hear from God when you are tired. Give Him the best part of your day, be that morning or night. My best time for Him is around 6 A.M. My wife's is about 18 hours later. Our Lord God is the priority in your marriage restoration, so He deserves your best.

Hopelessness - Do you doubt what God is telling you? Does it all seem impossible? Charlyne often writes about what Mary must have experienced when the angel announced that she, a virgin, would bear the Savior. You must remember that nothing is impossible with God.

Distraction - What is standing between you and hearing God's voice every day? Is it the opinion of others? The counsel of people? The circumstances? Negative comments? You must not become distracted by people, nor by what you are witnessing, in your search for God's perfect answers for you and your marriage situation.

Doubt - When life sees doubt, faith sees a way. Please learn to hear from God all day, every day, and in every way. Let it become a faith-building experience for you. Doubt and faith cannot occupy your heart at the same time very well.

Deceit - The enemy will also attempt to give you his evil direction. A vital part of growing into a solid, mature Christian, walking with Jesus Christ, is to develop discernment, so that you can know the difference.

*The man without the Spirit does not accept the things that come from the Spirit of God, for they are foolishness to him, and he cannot understand them, because they are spiritually discerned. The spiritual man makes judgments about all things, but he himself is not subject to any man's judgment. **I Corinthians 2:14-15***

Hearing the voice of God throughout your day is a mystery. It is supernatural, but at the same time, it is not complicated. You and I need only to block the hindrances and align with God to hear His counsel and His direction.

Charlyne and I pray that you may overcome the busyness, the tiredness, the hopelessness, the distraction, the doubt, and the deceit, so that you may soon make life's journey, listening to the Lord (alone) for every decision, both large and small.

My sheep listen to my voice; I know them, and they follow me. I give them eternal life, and they shall never perish; no one can snatch them out of my hand. ***John 10:27-28***

TOGETHER

Flee from sexual immorality. All other sins a man commits are outside his body, but he who sins sexually sins against his own body. Do you not know that your body is a temple of the Holy Spirit, who is in you, whom you have received from God? You are not your own. ***1 Corinthians 6:18-19***

The daily *Charlyne Cares* messages are written to encourage you. The Holy Spirit leads us to instruct you, not in the Rejoice way, nor in the Steinkamp way, but in the Lord's way, as given to all of us in the Bible, our manual for life and for living.

Thousands of people subscribe to our daily email devotional. That number can be divided into two groups. In one group, people are just along for the ride. They receive so much marriage restoration email they do not even know what they receive. This group, sadly, is looking for the restoration of their marriage in a computer, not in Christ. Many people have mastered the language of standing, but they do not know the love of standing. Those men and women are doing little less than waiting to see if somehow their spouse wanders back home. They may do so, but unless hearts are changed, they will never stay home *"till death do us part."*

How we wish those people were like the second group: men and women who are sold out to Jesus Christ and will do anything to make certain their lives are 100% aligned with His will and His way. Unlike the first group, who want to see how close to the line they can live, this second group strives to see how close to Christ they can live.

We once asked a question in the Rejoice CyberPoll that said, "Did you and your spouse live together before marriage?" **41% of the respondents replied yes.**

Every day we receive email that reads, "My husband/wife and I have been married for X years, but we have been together for Y years." Even though the writer admits to having lived together before marriage, it is very seldom that these emails contain any comment about the stander's repentance for having lived in sin, often for years.

If you have "been together" before marriage in a living arrangement with your spouse, or with anyone else, and you have confessed that sin to God and asked for His forgiveness, we commend you. If you have never dealt with prior immoral living arrangements as sin, we encourage you to do that today.

Perhaps no one told you at the time that such an arrangement was sin. Nevertheless, studies have shown that couples who lived together before marriage have a much smaller chance of making their marriages work. Once you have asked forgiveness from God through the shed Blood of Jesus, those studies are all out the window.

My people are destroyed for lack of knowledge. . . **Hosea 4:6 (NKJV)**

The bottom line is that sex outside of marriage, before marriage, during marriage (with another person), is a sin. With sin in your life, your prayers for marriage restoration or for anything else are being blocked. That is not the idea of some straight-laced Steinkamp, but of our Lord God.

Do you not know that the wicked will not inherit the kingdom of God? Do not be deceived: Neither the sexually immoral nor idolaters nor adulterers nor male prostitutes nor homosexual offenders nor thieves nor the greedy nor drunkards nor slanderers nor swindlers will inherit the kingdom of God. **I Corinthians 6:9**

The body is not meant for sexual immorality, but for the Lord, and the Lord for the body. **1 Corinthians 6:13b**

Put to death, therefore, whatever belongs to your earthly nature: sexual immorality, impurity, lust, evil desires and greed, which is idolatry. Because of these, the wrath of God is coming. **Colossians 3:5-6**

This message is being typed on a Saturday. Tonight is the night that many refer to as "date night." Many prodigals will be breaking the hearts of their spouse tonight as they go out on dates. Some prodigals who still live at home will be sneaking out to meet someone other than their spouse.

It will shock that second group of sold-out standers mentioned above to hear that a few people in the first group, who call themselves standers, will be going out on dates tonight. They are more concerned with their happiness than with their holiness, which is God's concern. When a stander goes out with someone of the opposite sex, for any reason, it is temptation from the enemy and always means trouble, unless someone repents.

It is our goal that nothing, absolutely nothing, blocks God's restoration of your marriage. If sexual sins, past or present, are hanging over you, we pray that today you will make things right before our Holy God. If you are being tempted by the attentions of someone else, we pray that God will give you the strength to do what is right.

Are we pushing the panic button prematurely? Not at all. For reasons of confidentiality we cannot disclose details, but people who were once standing for their marriage have given up and a few have even mumbled marriage vows to someone else. Many of these relationships started out with "just a friend" when the stander who was involved knew better.

Let's imagine that one evening you have gone out for dinner. Across the room from you sits your pastor and a woman who is not his wife. There's nothing happening. They are just sitting together and enjoying each other's company. The pastor's wife is not there, only your man of God and another woman. What would you think? Who would you tell? Would your opinion of your pastor be helped or harmed?

When later confronted with what you saw, the pastor defends, "She's just a friend." What would you think? What would your friends or your spouse think if you use the same justification? Would their sighting of you in the company of someone other than your spouse help or hinder your witness as a stander?

It is something to think about.

So, if you think you are standing firm, be careful that you don't fall! No temptation has seized you except what is common to man. And God is faithful; he will not let you be tempted beyond what you can bear. But when you are tempted, he will also provide a way out so that you can stand up under it. **1 Corinthians 10:12-13**

HAVE YOU DILUTED YOUR STAND?

Will he find delight in the Almighty? Will he call upon God at all times? "I will teach you about the power of God; the ways of the Almighty I will not conceal. You have all seen this yourselves. Why then this meaningless talk?" **Job 27:10-12**

Charlyne tries to always keep a jug of iced tea in our refrigerator. By the end of the week, when the tea is almost gone, water can be added to increase what is in the jug. Just before grocery day, more water may be added. The jug's contents still look like iced tea, but it does not taste like true iced tea because it's primarily water.

Have you diluted your stand for marriage restoration God's way with other things, until what remains today looks like a stand, but the power is diluted? To be honest, diluting God's way of handling marriage problems with the world's way is more like mixing oil and water than mixing water and iced tea. It makes a mess.

Charlyne and I are well aware how tempting and easy it is for the best of standers to dilute their stands. Jack and Jill separated after Jack fell into sin. Someone introduced Jill to Jesus. Soon she had a growing relationship with her Savior. Things were happening in Jack's life, both seen and unseen, as Jill prayed and read God's Word. She saw her small prayers being answered. Jill had promise after promise, from God's Word, that He would heal their marriage. She kept a journal and listened to audio teaching. Praise music filled her home 24 hours a day. Yes, Jill had her moments of tears, but even greater, she felt the presence of the Holy Spirit surrounding her, protecting her and guiding her.

Then one day when Jack was not living at home, Jill started having thoughts. "No one should have to put up with stuff like Jack is doing!" As was her custom, Jill took it before the Lord in prayer. She waited and waited, but God seemed not to answer her repeated pleas to Him. Being a young Christian, Jill wanted instant results and she was not receiving them.

Jill returned to the computer and searched for "Stop Divorce." There was no need to ask God, nor Jesus, nor the Holy Spirit, because Jill thought in error that they had failed her. She clicked on a site that "promised" to help get her Jack home. They even boasted about their high success rate. Jill had just opened the tap that was about to dilute her stand with God for marriage restoration.

In the following days, Jill explored more sites from that list. She even discovered sites where she could share with the world what Jack had done. Soon people around the world were offering their advice. Soon the advice of people became louder to Jill than the voice of God. In fact, the time Jill once spent in the Bible and prayer was replaced with chat rooms and bulletin boards. Yes, some of the replies were crude, and a few even mentioned God, but her new friends answered so much quicker than God.

In time, Jill wrote the marriage ministry that had helped her so much in the beginning, lamenting how God had failed her and how she was giving up her stand. She could not tell God directly, because she no longer talked with Him, nor did she wait for His Word. Why read an outdated Bible when people online had already read it and seemed to have all the answers? God seemed a far-off stranger, when her friends with online advice were always there. Before long, Jill's conversations online sounded more like the *"Before Christ"* Jill than the *"Redeemed"* Jill.

If you have been where Jill is right now, you might know the rest of the story. When Jack found a counterfeit replacement for Jill, she privately gave up on marriage restoration. To her friends, she was still a stander, but by now, to Jill "standing" meant, "If Jack ever wanders home, and if he meets my conditions, I might consider allowing him to come back." Jill gave little thought to Jack's eternal destiny or to their one-flesh marriage.

By the time Jack, like the prodigal son, "came to his senses," Jill no longer wanted him home. Jill raised the bar to Jack's coming back in the front door higher than Jack could jump. She had head knowledge of standing for marriage restoration, but her heart knowledge had been diluted by dabbling in the world's ways until it was useless.

What did God think?

As an aside, the bar across our front door prohibiting me from coming home was always low. It was so low that some misunderstanding people called my wife a "doormat." In truth, Charlyne was just being like Jesus. He loved me so much that He went to the cross and died for me. Imagine the Man without sin, dying to pay for the sin I committed. Yet He did not have a high bar for me to receive His gift of eternal life. He said simply, "Come unto me." My wife said simply, "Come home." She trusted God, Jesus, and the Holy Spirit to convict me of the wrong I was doing, and to make changes. Know what? Her ways (like His ways) work!

Jack and Jill's story has a happy but painful ending. Others continued to pray for both Jack and Jill. Each went through much heartache, but God had not given up. There came a day when the Holy Spirit touched prodigal Jack, and by now, a nearly-prodigal Jill, and set marriage restoration into motion for one more couple.

How did it all start? Jill slightly diluted her stand with God with the things of the world. Once that spigot of the world is opened, it flows more and more.

How did it all end? By a movement of the Holy Spirit of God in Jack and Jill's lives, because people were praying, regardless of what they saw happening.

Charlyne and I pray that your stand is 100% pure. If you have diluted your stand, little or much, or if your hand is near the spigot, the Lord is waiting for you to fully come back to Him. As the hymn writer of yesteryear wrote, *"His Blood can cleanse your heart and make you free. His love can fill your soul, and you will see, 'twas best for Him to have His way with thee.'"*

This is the message we have heard from him and declare to you: God is light; in him there is no darkness at all. If we claim to have fellowship with him yet walk in the darkness, we lie and do not live by the truth. **1 John 1:5-6**

THE LORD'S HOSPITAL

Then they cried to the LORD in their trouble, and he saved them from their distress. He sent forth his word and healed them; he rescued them from the grave. **Psalm 107:19-20**

With all the current talk about healthcare in America, I thought about how much in common physical illness has with the spiritual illness of divorce that is attempting to destroy half of our marriages. Both physical illness and the spiritual illness in marriages are devastating, not only to the individuals involved, but also to entire families.

Have you ever noticed what happens when an individual relates their health problems to others? Someone always thinks they know the cure. The person may be a total stranger and few details are even known, yet they know exactly the right way to bring about healing.

How many times have good people who are serious about standing and praying for marriage restoration been sent in the wrong direction by a well-intended individual offering a hurting or abandoned spouse a couple of spiritual aspirins? The secret to seeing your marriage restored by God is in knowing whose aspirin to accept and whose to decline.

Our Lord God tells us in Scripture that He is our Great Physician. If God can heal our physical bodies, why do we doubt that He can answer our prayers and heal our marriages?

Praise the LORD, O my soul; all my inmost being, praise his holy name. Praise the LORD, O my soul, and forget not all his benefits - who forgives all your sins and heals all your diseases. **Psalm 103:1-3**

In November 1996, I had an appointment for testing at my doctor's office. That afternoon I thought I would be gone for about an hour. My desktop was a mess and I did not even turn off my computer. Instead of returning in an hour, I returned weeks later after admissions to two hospitals, brain surgery and other complications. My doctor saw something in my test that was life-threatening and needed immediate attention. Instead of returning to my messy desk, I was sent directly to the hospital.

In the days that followed, my wife who was being told to prepare for my death, cleaned up my desk and turned off my computer. Her faith was not in the wisdom of doctors, but in the Word of God. I praise Him today for a wife who did not give up on me when I became a prodigal; neither did she give up on me when Satan tried to steal my life through illness.

". . .Lord, the one you love is sick." When he heard this, Jesus said, "This sickness will not end in death. No, it is for God's glory so that God's Son may be glorified through it."
John 11:3-4

Charlyne and I hurt for what you are going through. We also hurt for your spouse, as well as your children and other family members who are being devastated by the current events in your home. This is not a time to play the blame game, but a time for you to seek help from the Great Physician.

Were Charlyne to ever call **9-1-1** for me, all she would have to say is "cardiac history" and "chest pain" to have help dispatched. No one would question what I had been doing that might have made it my fault that I had chest pain. In life or death situations, there is no time to play the blame game.

Our Lord God, the Great Physician, will not play the blame game when you sincerely cry out for His help. You might have been an inattentive mate. Being unfaithful to your spouse might have caused your problems. God does not care who was at fault, as long as we are willing to confess our sin and come to Him in our helpless condition.

"'Call to me and I will answer you and tell you great and unsearchable things you do not know.'" **Jeremiah 33:3**

Could it be that the Great Physician is going to admit you to His hospital for healing? Many people, starting with yours truly, bristle when a physician uses the term "hospital," but we acknowledge that some illnesses require hospitalization for healing.

I invite you to take a tour of the Lord's Hospital with me, where God often works His miracle of the healing that brings about marriage restoration.

Let's start with the **Admitting Department**. This is where many hurting men and women hear for the first time that God can heal hurting marriages. For some people, this is also where they find a personal relationship with Jesus Christ they had not previously known. In Admitting, a hospital learns about the person, and the person learns about the hospital. The only insurance card anyone will ever ask you for is actually an assurance that you do know Jesus, for that is central in marriage restoration God's way. No one is ever refused care at the Lord's Hospital.

That if you confess with your mouth, "Jesus is Lord" and believe in your heart that God raised him from the dead, you will be saved. **Romans 10:9**

In one sense, our Rejoice Pompano Bible studies serve as an Admitting Department for Rejoice Marriage Ministries. Those Monday night meetings are the first contact for many people searching for marriage care.

No one actually receives treatment for their condition from the Admitting Department. They do not heal people. Likewise, Charlyne and I do not heal marriages. Our responsibility is only to do the paperwork and pray for our God to heal families.

There is no question who your physician is at the Lord's Hospital. There is only one doctor on staff and that is the Great Physician. He may have many people helping, but He is the Healer.

When Jesus had entered Capernaum, a centurion came to him, asking for help. "Lord," he said, "my servant lies at home paralyzed and in terrible suffering." Jesus said to him, "I will go and heal him." **Matthew 8:5-7**

Jesus went throughout Galilee, teaching in their synagogues, preaching the good news of the kingdom, and healing every disease and sickness among the people. News about him spread all over Syria, and people brought to him all who were ill with various diseases, those suffering severe pain, the demon-possessed, those having seizures, and the paralyzed, and he healed them. **Matthew 4:23-24**

Some people are hurting so badly they can't come through the Admitting Department and are instead rushed through the hospital's **Emergency Department,** a place set up to provide urgent life-saving care. Every once in a while we will hear a report of a person who has died outside of a well-equipped emergency room. For different reasons, they balked at going inside and receiving the help they needed. Being near the Emergency Department but not becoming a patient might be likened to a person in a hurting marriage who looks at God's help from a distance, but never trusts Him to heal their marriage.

My wife and I hurt when we hear of a stander who cannot totally step out of the world into God's presence in seeking their marriage restoration. Just like the patient who dies in the hospital parking lot, they both know where help can be found, but remain outside. In both situations, there are sad consequences.

As you seek marriage restoration help and healing at the Lord's Hospital, one of the stops will be in the **X-ray Department**. God already knows what is going on inside of you, but an x-ray will allow you to see what is damaged and where healing is needed.

Test me, O LORD, and try me, examine my heart and my mind. **Psalm 26:2**

"'...This is what the LORD, the God of your father David, says: I have heard your prayer and seen your tears; I will heal you.'" **2 Kings 20:5**

Blood is the lifeline of the human body. Through it, oxygen is carried to each cell. At the Lord's Hospital, the **Blood Bank** is critical. The only blood donor was Jesus Christ, who was crucified for my sins and for yours. His blood is sufficient to cover everything you have ever done, so that God will not count your sins against you. Once you have confessed and repented, you have access to His royal blood.

But now in Christ Jesus you who once were far away have been brought near through the blood of Christ. **Ephesians 2:13**

Many people who enter the Lord's Hospital discover that **surgery** is necessary. The Great Physician wants to remove from you anything that would be harmful to your walk as a Christian or to your marriage. There is no second opinion needed, because the Great Physician created your body. He gave you life, and He has a plan and a purpose for you and for your marriage. We never get in trouble if we follow Him and always do what He says to do.

"'I will give you a new heart and put a new spirit in you; I will remove from you your heart of stone and give you a heart of flesh. And I will put my Spirit in you and move you

to follow my decrees and be careful to keep my laws.'"
Ezekiel 36:26-27

Speaking of getting into trouble, some stander patients in the Lord's Hospital have trouble when they get caught in the *"his/her marriage is restored, but I sought God's help first"* criticism. God knows what He is doing. Your marriage will be restored when everyone is ready. Please do not place demands on the Great Physician for He knows what is best. He always makes rounds at the Lord's Hospital at the right time.

By this stage of your treatment at the Lord's Hospital, you have received many **IVs** of nutrients and medication to help your marriage heal. It is always good news during a hospitalization for the doctor to say the IV can come out. After it does, you have a personal responsibility to keep good things going into your body. You need to keep taking in Scriptures every day, all week long.

For the word of God is living and active. Sharper than any double-edged sword, it penetrates even to dividing soul and spirit, joints and marrow; it judges the thoughts and attitudes of the heart. Nothing in all creation is hidden from God's sight. Everything is uncovered and laid bare before the eyes of him to whom we must give account. **Hebrews 4:12-13**

It seems the Great Physician frequently orders **stress testing** for those who turn to Him. It is not because the Lord is punishing us, but He is helping us to grow as Christians. The goal is for each of us to learn to depend on Him to carry us through everything we face.

Some of the most upbeat people in any hospital can be found in the **Physical Therapy Department** as they encourage healing patients to regain lost functions. They teach the proper way to handle everyday tasks and at the same time stress safety. The Lord's Hospital is no exception. Even after your discharge, God may keep you coming back for outpatient therapy, with a favorite pastor or Bible teacher as your encourager. He will push you to become all that you can be for Christ, instruct you how to live out the Christian life day by day, and teach you to be on guard when the enemy attempts to trip you up.

Another busy area in the Lord's Hospital is the **Pain Clinic**. There is no medicine that can take away pain like our Lord God. Most of the patients at the Lord's Hospital are suffering deeply from the pain of abandonment. Many also have flare-ups of rejection. Regardless of what kind of pain you are suffering today, be it physical, emotional or spiritual, the Great Physician is ready to cure your pain problem.

Some people who contact us at Rejoice Marriage Ministries are spiritually dehydrated. They are depending on one stay in the Lord's Hospital to keep them going spiritually until their spouse is home and saved. They are taking nothing in from prayer, Bible reading, and time alone with God, leaving them dried up. These people are susceptible to catching diseases such as: *Givingupitis, Toohardism,* or the *Someonebetter Syndrome.* Thankfully, the entire family of discouragement diseases is easily and quickly treated by the Great Physician, but only if the patient follows His instructions.

Visiting hours at the Lord's Hospital are unlimited. There will constantly be people stopping by to see how you are handling this disease of marriage problems or divorce. They especially will be watching how closely you follow the Great Physician's instructions.

When I was a prodigal spouse, one of the far countries where I resided for a season was a small rural community with one hospital. Since everyone in town seemed to know everyone else, a person would not go to the hospital to visit just one person, but would end up visiting several people.

The visitor could give an update on practically everyone in the hospital, how well they were doing or how fast they were failing. People are watching you, even when you may not be aware of it. May you always be found holding fast to the Great Physician.

A BLOOPER BLESSING

From the fullness of his grace we have all received one blessing after another. For the law was given through Moses; grace and truth came through Jesus Christ. **John 1:16-17**

When people send us their testimonies and praises, they are often filled with typos and other errors. Throughout the week, we work on excerpts from testimonies for the following Saturday's *Charlyne Cares*. Along the way we attempt to correct the errors, though we still miss a few. Early one morning I was tempted to leave one testimony error just as it had been sent to us.

A stander had shared about a positive contact with her absent husband. In the last sentence, she must have intended to type **"God is so good,"** but she left out one letter. She had typed instead, **"God is so God."**

Granted, God is so good. None of us can count the blessings He has bestowed upon us, if we would only stop to reflect on them. For too many standers, the glass of God's goodness is half empty, instead of half full. Yes, you have a major marriage problem, but can't you see the mighty hand of God providing for you all along life's way? Yes, there may be health problems, as there has been for our family. There may be financial problems or job problems or legal problems, but I pray you are keeping your eyes open to witness the rainbows of blessings the Lord always brings in the midst of the storms.

God is so good, but as that writer shared today, God is so God. To me, that means you and I can depend on God, trusting in the promises from His Word, regardless of the circumstances.

Do you realize that God is the only one who cannot fail you today? You could lose your job, have your health fail you, people forsake you, or a myriad of other tragedies happen, but God will still be God through it all. He never changes.

Even though it happened a long time ago and is now insignificant, a specific event keeps coming to my mind as I type. Many years ago, in my pre-prodigal days, I served on our church board. Our long-time and beloved pastor called a special board meeting on a Saturday afternoon. At that meeting, he stunned all of us by giving his resignation. The thought of his leaving was so far-fetched that Charlyne thought I was joking when I arrived home and told her.

During that pastor's leaving, I came to realize that God is so God. In my eyes, a man who was close to me was failing me, as well as many others, by leaving. I had to understand that pastor was not taking God with him when he left. I had been trusting in a man, not in a God who is so God.

What person do you trust most in today? Hopefully, it is not Bob or Charlyne, because we may let you down. Your professional counselor may retire or relocate. For most of us, we will lose our parents to death before we are called home. Your prayer partner or best friend may be removed. Like what happened to me, a special man of God may leave. Legal decisions can be reversed. What will you do then? The only One you can trust in with full confidence that they will always be there, never changing, never disappointing you, is Jesus.

Look at the people of the Old Testament. Time and time again, everyone and everything around them failed, but God was so God to them. From Abraham, ready to sacrifice his son, to childless Abraham and Sarah, to Daniel in the lion's den, to the three men in the furnace, we witness over and over throughout the Bible, that God is so God.

It thrills me to know that the same God who led the Israelites through the wilderness wants to lead you and me through today. The same God who protected Jonah in the belly of a whale is offering His protection to you and me. The same God who raised Lazarus from the dead also raised our dead marriage. He wants to do the same for you, if you will allow His Son, Jesus, to take full control of you and your life.

Yes, God is so good, but God is also God. Does He have His rightful place in your life and in your mess of a marriage, or has He quietly been replaced, one step at a time, by other things, other people, other activities? Satan, the enemy of our soul, does not do that all at once, but instead by one insignificant subtle step at a time.

Let's not forget that God is so God. As the hymn writer expressed so well, *"My hope is built on nothing less than Jesus blood and righteousness, I dare not trust the sweetest frame, but wholly lean on Jesus' name. His oath, His covenant, His blood, support me in the whelming flood. When all around my soul gives way, He then is all my Hope and Stay. (Refrain): On Christ the solid Rock I stand; All other ground is sinking sand; All other ground is sinking sand."* (Song-Public Domain)

Don't be deceived, my dear brothers. Every good and perfect gift is from above, coming down from the Father of the heavenly lights, who does not change like shifting shadows. **James 1:16-17**

SATAN'S SECRET WEAPON

Create in me a pure heart, O God, and renew a steadfast spirit within me. Do not cast me from your presence or take your Holy Spirit from me. Restore to me the joy of your salvation and grant me a willing spirit, to sustain me.
Psalm 51:10-11

One of the most destructive tools that the enemy uses to thwart marriage restoration is one of his most subtle. It creeps up to ensnare not only men and women who are praying for marriage restoration, but also couples who are back together again and working through the process of marriage restoration. It is not one of the three A's of alcohol, adultery or abuse, because they are so obvious. Satan delights in using that which is not so obvious to destroy not only families and marriages, but also individuals.

Like so many other areas that Satan uses, this one has been endorsed by modern society as acceptable. I am writing about the relationship between one married spouse (or stander) and a member of the opposite sex.

We know standers who would never consider being inappropriate in any way with a member of the opposite sex. Yet sometimes they can see nothing wrong with close opposite sex friendships, even to the extent of going out with the other sex. After all, "We're just friends."

I cannot overstate how Satan desires to use your naive actions regarding your relationship with other people against you. Beyond that, you need to remember that anyone who is going through separation and divorce is vulnerable. Regardless of how strong you are in your Christian beliefs, rejection by your spouse combined with flattery from a friend equals trouble.

Recently, I read a quote from a prominent pastor. He said that if he was driving in a rainstorm and passed a female member of his church without an umbrella, he would never consider stopping to pick her up because of what someone else might think seeing the two of them in a car together.

My opposite sex warning to you extends even to email relationship. Several years ago we received a frantic call from a female stander. She had developed an email friendship with a male stander several years' difference in age from her who lived over 2,000 miles away. The man had been reading something into the relationship that the woman never intended. He was ready to pack up and move to be near her. She was calling to see what she should do. "What she should do," was not to have chosen to carry on an email correspondence with a man. The last we heard, neither marriage was restored, and neither person continued to stand.

The time that two people spend together builds familiarity. As a friendship with a member of the opposite sex strengthens over time, that person starts to look better, while the view of their own covenant spouse for whom they are standing starts to grow out of focus.

You might think that Charlyne and I are being old-fashioned in this matter, but over the years we have seen scores of marriages lose hope of ever being restored because a once-standing spouse thought they were different and could handle an opposite sex friendship without it ever becoming a relationship.

If there was one thing that Charlyne and I could tell you that we have learned in the past 20 years of marriage ministry, it would be that opposite sex friendships while standing for marriage restoration do not work. We have seen prodigals who were close to coming home go the opposite direction because of the way events involving their spouse were interpreted. We know standers who simply gave up because their spouse looked so bad compared to another person. In many of these instances, by the time the stander comes to their senses, their spouse is long gone, never to be heard from again.

After a prodigal returns is not the time for their mate to break off innocent opposite-sex relationships. They never should have been allowed to form in the first place. If I had come home on the afternoon we suddenly remarried and that evening Charlyne received a couple of phone calls from men she said were "just friends," one more huge obstacle would have been added to our restoration process.

If you are serious about marriage restoration, there is no room for a person of the opposite sex in your life. That includes prayer partners, co-workers outside the job, coffee friends, email groups, people on Facebook, neighbors, old friends and any other justification a stander might attempt to use. I can promise you that Satan will eventually use that relationship to harm either you or your hopes of marriage restoration.

Rejoice Marriage Ministries Inc. does not have rules that we demand standers follow to be part of this Ministry. We do have suggestions that the test of time has proven to help or hinder the permanent restoration of a marriage by God. Foremost among these is the concept that standers need to socialize and cultivate friendships only among people of the same sex.

Look at the scenario of a hypothetical couple where the man is the stander and whose marriage has been gloriously restored by God. A few years later, that husband and wife go out to dinner. A woman approaches their table and warmly greets the man with comments about how long it has been since she has seen him. The wife does not know this woman and is basically ignored until the husband awkwardly introduces them. After the woman has gone on her way, the wife inquires as to who she was. The husband says that she was a member of the stander's group that he attended while praying for his wife to come home.

The next question from that wife will be, "Did you date?" The man confesses that he and the woman had gone out for coffee a couple of times. At the time of the coffee klatches, everything was above board. However, Satan made an entry to try again later to destroy this marriage.

At home that evening, the returned wife is unsettled over meeting the other woman she did not know about. Her husband is about to be grilled for details. In his sincerity, he admits that he and the other woman had gone to a couple of movies together while both were standing. The enemy has just kicked the wheels of doubt and mistrust into action in that wife's mind.

She demands to know how much the woman knew about their problems. In an attempt to be totally honest, the husband confesses they used to email back and forth about each other's problems and had a few phone conversations.

The restoration process of that couple has suffered a setback, all over what appeared to be nothing, but happened when a standing husband could see nothing wrong with having an opposite sex friend. You can be assured the incident at the restaurant will come up over and over again when that couple has strife between them.

How could this have all been avoided? By a stander being firm on having only same-sex friends. We have seen some variation of the above scenario repeated time and time again during the life of this Ministry. A marriage is always the loser. Charlyne and I pray that, for the sake of your family, you will make an evaluation of your opposite sex friendships before it is too late for your marriage.

TWO WAYS TO TRAVEL

"I will lead the blind by ways they have not known, along unfamiliar paths I will guide them; I will turn the darkness into light before them and make the rough places smooth. These are the things I will do; I will not forsake them."
Isaiah 42:16

Each year after Easter has passed we are just ending the tourist season. The people we call "snowbirds" are going back to their northern homes after escaping to Florida for the winter. Some communities will lose 50% of their population until it gets cold again up north.

Year round Floridians joke that cities up north must have contests and send their worst drivers to Florida for the winter. With many of the visitors being elderly, we witness some amazing things in traffic each winter. We witness out-of-state cars backing up on I-95 when an exit has been passed. Our winter friends stop in traffic to read road maps. They frequently ask for directions and are known to make turns across multiple lanes of traffic. Each year we hear of tourists making fatal turns into canals.

One Saturday I was watching a church service being re-broadcast on the Internet. I heard a unique song that reminded me of Florida tourists. Even greater, it reminded me of men and women praying and standing with God for marriage restoration. I have no idea of the song title, but its lyrics told of a person at the intersection of Heartbreak Ridge and New Hope Road.

In my mind's eye, I could envision a car full of tourists, with a confused and perplexed driver trying to decide which way to go, while everyone in the car offered suggestions.

Even more, I could envision an abandoned and hurting spouse having to make a decision between continuing on rugged Heartbreak Ridge or making a turn onto New Hope Road, a smoother road, but a new way to travel. Everyone around them seemed to have a different opinion on which way to go. The majority of other spouses seemed to be continuing on Heartbreak Ridge, full well knowing it leads to divorce, but hoping the traveling would become smoother afterward.

New Hope Road was not at all crowded, despite being a much smoother road. Some were hesitant to turn onto that road because they did not know how long that journey might be. Even if a long trip followed, it would be a peaceful journey. New Hope Road had signs all along the way from God Himself, promising His presence with those who traveled on His New Hope Road.

Not everyone stayed on the road they had chosen. Some people started on Heartbreak Ridge, but while on that journey, they changed over to New Hope Road. Others started out on New Hope Road but later made a U-turn to go back to Heartbreak Ridge. Once on Heartbreak Ridge, many later had deep regrets.

If you were driving to South Florida for a visit, most likely you would be coming south on either I-95 or the Florida Turnpike. About a hundred miles north of us, in Fort Pierce, FL those roads come close to each other. The next time they meet is another 50 miles south in Jupiter, FL. The trip on I-95 is 12 miles longer than the same trip on the Turnpike. When I-95 was being planned, one county negotiated to have the road run through the western part of their county. In fact, if you were driving south on the stretch of the Interstate, at one point the compass would report you were briefly traveling north.

Floridians who know about the two highways pay the toll and travel on the turnpike, shaving a dozen miles from their journey. In return, they drive on a fairly straight, well patrolled highway with call boxes every mile.

When a marriage is falling apart and a wounded spouse finds themself at the intersection of Heartbreak Ridge and New Hope Road, they face a decision. Travel on Heartbreak Ridge is free, except for the emotional cost, while there is a price to pay for traveling New Hope Road or at least so it seems at the beginning of the journey. People who take New Hope Road are often considered odd by their family and friends. God may not have revealed to others what He has revealed to the person taking the journey from Miserable Marriage to Restoration City.

My friend, where are you today? Have you been forced onto Heartbreak Ridge against your will and are now at the intersection of New Hope Road and trying to decide which way to go? Travel far enough on Heartbreak Ridge and you will someday discover that it comes to a dead end long before you ever reach home.

*There is a way that seems right to a man, but in the end it leads to death. **Proverbs 14:12***

Unless you turn off of Heartbreak Ridge, the death of your troubled marriage is inevitable.

*"Enter through the narrow gate. For wide is the gate and broad is the road that leads to destruction, and many enter through it. But small is the gate and narrow the road that leads to life, and only a few find it." **Matthew 7:13-14***

If you turn onto New Hope Road with the destination of a restored marriage, your Lord God who created you promises to guide you every mile of the way.

*When Jesus spoke again to the people, he said, "I am the light of the world. Whoever follows me will never walk in darkness, but will have the light of life." **John 8:12***

Have you ever seen an airport or congested area where a vehicle is sent out to lead others to their destination? Those vehicles often have a large sign that reads **"Follow Me."** You are approaching a crossroads just ahead and Jesus is saying "Follow Me." My wife and I pray that you will follow Jesus in His narrow way. That is the real way home.

Since you are my rock and my fortress, for the sake of your name lead and guide me. Free me from the trap that is set for me, for you are my refuge. **Psalm 31:3-4**

THE PRODIGAL'S FOREMOST DESIRE

But how is it to your credit if you receive a beating for doing wrong and endure it? But if you suffer for doing good and you endure it, this is commendable before God. To this you were called, because Christ suffered for you, leaving you an example, that you should follow in his steps.
1 Peter 2:20-21

Charlyne has a unique style in her radio teaching in that she asks questions. The Holy Spirit uses her questions to draw out answers from within the listener. When I was editing a CD for her, Charlyne asked nineteen questions in four minutes. Somehow, her many questions all fit together to create another great *"God Heals Hurting Marriages"* radio program.

Nevertheless, I reminded Charlyne that she was asking a lot of questions. "Are you giving answers?" I challenged. Less than twenty four hours later, I was reading and came across a comment regarding how Jesus often used questions in His teaching. My wife was unknowingly teaching like Jesus.

May I borrow from Charlyne's style today and ask you a question? What do prodigals want? I do not ask why prodigals leave home, because we all know that answer. Husbands and wives walk out on their mates and their children because of an attack from the enemy. Drugs, sex, and alcohol are not "why" prodigals leave, but "how" they leave. You and I both know how temporal those pleasures can be, and so does every prodigal spouse. We make that discovery the hard way by experience, often at the cost of family, career, health and happiness.

What do prodigals want? More specifically, what does your prodigal spouse want from you? It can be summed up in one word: consistency. Are you, as a stander, living a consistent life before the Lord and also before your prodigal spouse?

One sentence from a testimony email comes to mind. A stander told of good contacts with her husband and then added, "He said he was proud of the way I was seeking good employment and getting my life together."

What is consistency? The dictionary says, "Firm coherence in applying principles or policy." In simpler words, it is doing the same things in the same, predictable way.

May I use Charlyne as an illustration? (Now I am even writing like she teaches!) Before we were remarried, I made deliberate attempts to push her buttons. Someone recently asked what that phrase means. In short, I was throwing tests at my wife in an attempt to get her to react in an unpredictable way. Had she done so, I could have shouted, "I told you! You are the same old Charlyne, with the same attitude, and still have the same old problems. Nothing has changed. Why would I want to come home to what I left?" I would have had a good excuse for not doing what God was telling me to do, namely to go home.

Regardless, of what I tested Charlyne with, she responded in the same way: with unconditional love. Despite how I put Charlyne to the test, in my double-minded state, she remained consistent. The situations she faced were not simple. Some involved the other woman. Charlyne never flinched, even though now I know how her heart was breaking. Finally I reasoned, as best as a prodigal can, that it would not be so bad to be remarried to her. That is when I surrendered to the wooing of the Holy Spirit.

During the past twenty-plus years of ministry, we have reminded standers of the basics in consistency that their mates are seeking. We have suggested that men get jobs. We have hinted to women they need to get their homes in order. I did not want to come home from a pig pen, nor to a pig pen. Our children, although wounded, had not been allowed to go wild while Mom was busy praying for marriage restoration.

"I will have time to straighten my life out and become consistent before my spouse comes home." No, you will not. Charlyne teaches often about the "suddenly" part of standing and marriage restoration. It is a lesson she knows well. On July 7, 1987, she left home to go to work as a divorced stander. That evening she came home a remarried woman.

Jesus Christ is our example for consistency. Even when the enemy tempted Him, Jesus did not waiver. He is consistent in opening His nail-pierced hands to all who come to Him in repentance. Jesus is consistent in being the Advocate before our Father God.

Do you get it? The prodigal lifestyle is a study in inconsistency. How often we prodigals move, change jobs, change "lovers," and change our minds. The only consistency in the pig pen is inconsistency. When the stench in our pig pen gets overpowering, due to our inconsistency, we prodigals start to look for consistency. That is best found in Jesus and in our standing mates.

I pray that today you will start the process, be it ever so slow, to develop a consistent life. That is what your prodigal wants. Remember, your beloved is not listening to how loud you shout about faith and change. The one you love is watching how straight you walk.

"I have set you an example that you should do as I have done for you. I tell you the truth, no servant is greater than his master, nor is a messenger greater than the one who sent him. Now that you know these things, you will be blessed if you do them." **John 13:15-17**

POWERLESS

O Hope of Israel, its Savior in times of distress, why are
you like a stranger in the land, like a traveler who stays
only a night? Why are you like a man taken by surprise,
like a warrior powerless to save? You are among us, O
LORD, and we bear your name; do not forsake us!
Jeremiah 14:8-9

You might know the feeling our daughter, Lori,
experienced before she had even left her driveway.
Everyone was in the van. Seat belts were on, doors locked.
Then instead of the engine coming to life, there was only a
series of recognizable clicks. Lori had a dead battery.

Possibly more plans are changed as a result of being
powerless than for any other reason. When the car battery
balks, we are powerless. When the cell phone battery is
used up, we are powerless. When the ATM keeps our bank
card, we are powerless. When the store does not have the
product we need, we are powerless. When the postman
says, "No mail," and we are expecting something
important, we are powerless. When we cannot log on to
download email, we are powerless. When the electricity
fails, we are powerless. There is no feeling more frustrating
than being powerless.

When your spouse says, "I am leaving and not coming
back," you are powerless—or are you? Men and women
feel and act like they are powerless when a mate abandons
them, but here's what the Bible says about the power of
God:

"But I have raised you up for this very purpose, that I
might show you my power and that my name might be
*proclaimed in all the earth." **Exodus 9:16***

210

"He did this so that all the peoples of the earth might know that the hand of the LORD is powerful and so that you might always fear the LORD your God." **Joshua 4:24**

"The Spirit of the LORD will come upon you in power, and you will prophesy with them; and you will be changed into a different person." **I Samuel 10:6**

David praised the LORD in the presence of the whole assembly, saying "Praise be to you, O LORD, God of our father Israel, from everlasting to everlasting. Yours, O LORD, is the greatness and the power and the glory and the majesty and the splendor, for everything in heaven and earth is yours. Yours, O LORD, is the kingdom; you are exalted as head over all." **1 Chronicles 29:10-11**

"To God belong wisdom and power; counsel and understanding are his." **Job 12:13**

Sing the glory of his name; make his praise glorious! Say to God, "How awesome are your deeds! So great is your power that your enemies cringe before you." **Psalm 66:2-3**

He determines the number of the stars and calls them each by name. Great is our Lord and mighty in power; his understanding has no limit. The LORD sustains the humble but casts the wicked to the ground. **Psalm 147:4-6**

"Praise be to the name of God for ever and ever; wisdom and power are his." **Daniel 2:20**

Jesus replied, "Are you not in error because you do not know the Scriptures or the power of God?" **Mark 12:24**

Jesus knew that the Father had put all things under his power, and that he had come from God and was returning to God;. . . **John 13:3**

"But you will receive power when the Holy Spirit comes on you; and you will be my witnesses in Jerusalem, and in all Judea and Samaria, and to the ends of the earth." Acts 1:8

By that evening Lori's husband, Scott, and her brother, Tim, put a new battery in the van. Lori and Scott were confident there was power in Lori's van to get her children to school the next morning. How about you? Do you trust in God's power for all you need this week and until your spouse comes home, or are you trusting in your own limited power?

In the past, I have seen motorists stranded with dead batteries who had their own jumper cables. All they needed to be on their way was a "jump." These people would connect their cables to their dead batteries, and then hold the other ends of the cables aloft. Soon a Good Samaritan would stop and offer a jump.

Do you feel powerless today? Are your spiritual and emotional batteries dead? Do not settle for walking and pushing through another day. Hold the jumper cables of your life aloft to the Lord today and watch how quickly you will receive power.

"O our God, will you not judge them? For we have no power to face this vast army that is attacking us. We do not know what to do, but our eyes are upon you." 2 Chronicles 20:12

YOU AND GOD ALONE

"This, then, is how you should pray: "'Our Father in heaven, hallowed be your name, your kingdom come, your will be done on earth as it is in heaven. Give us today our daily bread. Forgive us our debts, as we also have forgiven our debtors. And lead us not into temptation, but deliver us from the evil one.'" **Matthew 6:9-13**

Each morning as a new day starts, I can often tell where my wife has been in our home by the location of three old, crumbling pages. If they are in the kitchen, Charlyne has been there. If they are by her hair curler, I know that she has done her hair.

Almost a quarter of a century ago, when Charlyne began her stand, one of the many ways my wife prayed was by using a verse by verse breakdown of the Scripture passage we know as The Lord's Prayer. Her three typed pages give prayer guides for each phrase of those verses, including personalization with our names. After we were remarried in 1987, she continued to pray that passage each day. Several years ago I laminated them for her because they were literally falling apart from use.

May I give you an inside look at my wife's stand for a restored marriage and for my coming back to the Lord? Everything was centered around prayer and fasting. She had no Internet, received no email devotionals, and could afford to purchase only a minimal amount of what stander's material was available back then. She could count on one hand the number of times she met with other standers. She had one prayer partner, an older woman, with whom she shared details of our relationship. What she told Vera went to God's ears alone.

I am thankful my prodigal days happened back then, because I do not know where Charlyne and I would be today, considering what some people now call standing for marriage restoration. There were no chat rooms for "prayer requests" that are often nothing more than plain old gossip. Even though my parents lived only half a block from Charlyne, they went to their graves not knowing a lot of details about what I put my wife through. Charlyne did not "post" my activities with other women. The times when the circumstances had almost pushed her to give up were known by God alone.

Do you get it? It has to be you and God alone, without other people helping you make your decisions. If you will allow the Lord to be all you have, He will be all you need. What brought me home? The Holy Spirit did, in response to a wife's prayers and regardless of good or bad decisions she might have made when she did not hear God. It was not programs, people, pushing, pleading, or persuasion. It was a wife alone on her knees, in the presence of a Holy God, crying out and pleading for my soul to be saved from Hell.

Charlyne and I hurt each time a stander contacts us, asking for specific direction in their life. We hurt because we know that individual has missed the mark. They have not learned to listen to God and to Him alone.

Do you feel God cannot lead you in every situation? The Bible promises that He can.

Lead me, O LORD, in your righteousness because of my enemies - make straight your way before me. **Psalm 5:8**

Teach me your way, O LORD; lead me in a straight path because of my oppressors. **Psalm 27:11**

Since you are my rock and my fortress, for the sake of your name lead and guide me. **Psalm 31:3**

From the ends of the earth I call to you, I call as my heart grows faint; lead me to the rock that is higher than I. **Psalm 61:2**

Hear us, O Shepherd of Israel, you who lead Joseph like a flock; you who sit enthroned between the cherubim, shine forth. . . **Psalm 80:1**

Teach me to do your will, for you are my God; may your good Spirit lead me on level ground. **Psalm 143:10**

I guide you in the way of wisdom and lead you along straight paths. **Proverbs 4:11**

"In your unfailing love you will lead the people you have redeemed. In your strength you will guide them to your holy dwelling." **Exodus 15:13**

"Because of your great compassion you did not abandon them in the desert. By day the pillar of cloud did not cease to guide them on their path, nor the pillar of fire by night to shine on the way they were to take." **Nehemiah 9:19**

He restores my soul. He guides me in paths of righteousness for his name's sake. **Psalm 23:3**

Guide me in your truth and teach me, for you are God my Savior, and my hope is in you all day long. **Psalm 25:5**

He guides the humble in what is right and teaches them his way. **Psalm 25:9**

Since you are my rock and my fortress, for the sake of your name lead and guide me. **Psalm 31:3**

Send forth your light and your truth, let them guide me; let them bring me to your holy mountain, to the place where you dwell. **Psalm 43:3**

For this God is our God for ever and ever; he will be our guide even to the end. **Psalm 48:14**

May the nations be glad and sing for joy, for you rule the peoples justly and guide the nations of the earth. Selah.
Psalm 67:4

"The LORD will guide you always; he will satisfy your needs in a sun-scorched land and will strengthen your frame. You will be like a well-watered garden, like a spring whose waters never fail." **Isaiah 58:11**

"I will lead the blind by ways they have not known, along unfamiliar paths I will guide them; I will turn the darkness into light before them and make the rough places smooth. These are the things I will do; I will not forsake them." **Isaiah 42:16**

If you are having trouble hearing God and then trusting Him alone for every decision, please do a word study in your Bible on the word "trust." It is not that God can be trusted; God *must* be trusted to see marriages healed, people changed, and families restored.

Don't take another step in your stand without the net of our Lord Jesus and God's Word in place to give you support. If you are depending on people and programs to order your steps, there is a fall ahead. People may attempt to tell you where to place your foot, but only God can place it there for you.

May the God of hope fill you with all joy and peace as you trust in him, so that you may overflow with hope by the power of the Holy Spirit. **Romans 15:13**

BOOKENDS

They confronted me in the day of my disaster, but the LORD was my support. He brought me out into a spacious place; he rescued me because he delighted in me. **Psalm 18:18-19**

The bookends sitting on the shelf behind my desk have been a part of my life for about 45 years. Those two pyramid-shaped pieces of white polished stone were a gift from my parents in 1963 when I graduated from high school. One of the two bookends now has a chip, but they are not in bad condition, considering where they have been.

The bookends went to Cincinnati with me when I attended Mortuary Science College. When Charlyne and I married, those bookends moved to a new home, which was supposed to be for a lifetime. In 1974, after I had been called into the gospel ministry, the bookends traveled to Bible College, in the back of a rental truck with everything we owned. Sadly, those same bookends also left our home in 1985 and went with me to the far countries of life. After our remarriage, the bookends went right back on the same shelf from where they had started. After all of that, one small chip is not bad.

What do bookends do? Their task is uncomplicated. They simply hold upright a row of books. Have you ever considered what are the bookends of your stand for a restored marriage? In other words, what keeps your stand from tumbling? Just as my bookends may slide a bit from time to time and need to be tightened up and books straightened, both my bookends and your bookends will continue to stand.

On one end of your stand must be the bookend of God's Holy Word, the Bible. It is not the words of man, nor any ministry that will keep you standing. It must be the promises of God. On the opposite end of your stand must be your prayer life.

Charlyne has been asked hundreds of times, in one way or another, "What did you do to get Bob home?" She simply made certain that her bookends of Bible and prayer were always in place. There was absolutely nothing that I could place between her bookends that they could not support.

The current task of my bookends is to support a row of three-ring notebooks. There is one problem. The notebooks are an irregular size. The front is thicker than the back. As a result, the bookends tend to slide a bit more, but they still do their job holding up my irregular books.

Does your stand for a restored marriage, supported by the bookends of prayer and the Bible, have to hold up some irregular books right now? In recent months, we have seen an explosion in the number of standers forced to deal with their prodigal's non-covenant marriage to someone else or the birth of a child with the other person. Their bookends of standing are holding up some of the most irregular-sized books any marriage could be asked to endure.

Why are prodigals marrying others and having children in record number? Because the enemy thinks he knows what it will take to make you give up praying for your prodigal spouse. Is the evil one right? Let us stand together to prove him wrong. Resist thinking or saying, "If my husband/wife ever gets married/has a child with him/her, that's it! I am giving up!" You have just told Satan what it would take to make you quit standing.

Not only is the enemy now wanting that event to take place, the one you love is being pressured and manipulated into that situation. All of these "other people" feel that an adulterous marriage will cause you to give up. If that does not work, or if your spouse will not mumble words about marriage to them, someone suddenly becomes pregnant! I have never known a prodigal spouse who was excited to be planning the birth of a child. Somehow it just happens!

Are you going to allow the irregular books of non-covenant marriage or childbirth to topple your bookends? Charlyne and I pray that you will not, but will continue to allow God to be your Comforter during those events.

Following the death of my parents, I acquired a second set of bookends. They were my bronzed baby shoes from over 55 years ago. It is difficult to imagine that my present-day size thirteen feet ever fit into those tiny objects, but I know they did.

It may be difficult for you to imagine that your present baby steps in marriage restoration will ever grow into a family restored by God, but they will. If you keep those bookends of prayer and the Bible in place, you can stand, regardless of the irregular books the enemy attempts to add.

STANDER THERAPY

Trust in the Lord with all your heart and lean not on your own understanding; in all your ways acknowledge him, and he will make your paths straight. Do not be wise in your own eyes; fear the Lord and shun evil. This will bring health to your body and nourishment to your bones.
Proverbs 3:5-8

"Why don't I see anything happening in my marriage? I read all the testimonies I can find about marriage restoration, but nothing ever changes for me?" Does that describe your thoughts? If so, maybe it is time to start stander therapy; a program in which you will have an active part. God has given me an illustration comparing physical therapy with the stander therapy that every man or woman praying for a healed marriage must undergo.

I have shared previously about two strokes that left me paralyzed on my entire left side. (But each time that was only temporary until God moved.) I could not even wiggle a finger or toe, despite how hard I tried. After much work and negotiating with insurance companies on Charlyne's part, I was transferred to a physical rehabilitation unit. I attended therapy sessions four or five hours a day. Physical therapists worked on my leg. Occupational therapists did the same for my arm. A speech therapist worked with my memory and garbled speech.

If you have ever undergone physical therapy, you know that your physical therapist can be your best friend and your worst enemy all rolled into one person. They give you encouragement, but they also give correction.

Another truth about physical therapy is that no one recovers only by reading success stories of others. You could read my story of successful physical therapy, learning to walk all over again two times, but if you were paralyzed, my testimony would do little except encourage you. It would be necessary for you to do the exercises, over and over again, day after day, hour after hour most often with no one around until you were walking.

After my physical therapy sessions, I would be wheeled back to my hospital room, with sheets of instructions beside me. These were the exercises I had to do, on my own, until the next time I saw the therapist.

I think it would be safe to compare your daily *Charlyne Cares* with those exercise sheets. It is not my wife's intent to live out your life for you, but to give you the spiritual instruction that will allow you to first have a personal relationship with Jesus, and then to learn (by doing) how to hear from Him and depend on Him for your day to day answers.

After five days of rehab, we were seeing no results. On Saturday morning, an upbeat physical therapist and an assistant came into my room. I knew from the belts that he carried that we were going somewhere. "Let's get you up, Bob," he announced. "We're taking you down to the gym. It's time to go shopping."

The hospital's physical therapy gym was located on the second floor. The sunshine of a bright Florida spring day streamed in the huge windows. The beauty only reminded me of what I would be missing for the rest of my life. I couldn't walk. I couldn't use my arm or hand. I couldn't talk clearly. My memory was damaged.

Randy rolled my wheelchair over to the most helpful physical therapy device that I have ever used: an old grocery cart. "We'll need to teach you how to use a grocery cart, because it looks like you enjoy eating," he teased. My balance had been affected and I had a great fear of falling. Somehow, Randy's confident manner reassured me that I would be safe, even though he was about a foot shorter than me.

With one therapist holding the front of the cart, two others helped lift me from the wheelchair. Randy took his place on a rolling stool behind me. They placed my dangling left hand up on the bar of that basket. With therapists and assistants on all four sides of me, Randy commanded, "All right, big boy, it's time to walk!"

I cannot tell you how it was accomplished, but Randy would hold my limp leg rigid. I would take a step with my strong leg, Randy would shuffle the weak leg a couple inches, and the process would be repeated. I had my own four-member cheering squad with each step that I took. I was so excited that my left hand would fall unnoticed from the bar of the cart. One of the four would silently reposition it for me.

I have no idea how long we "shopped," but after I went back into the wheelchair, Randy measured the distance and proudly announced that I had walked 83 feet! I could not wait for Charlyne to arrive and hear about my shopping trip.

What distance does the Lord record that you have walked for Him? Randy did not expect me to get up and run a marathon. Neither does God expect you to start off running. He only wants you to be obedient, to get out of that wheelchair, and be obedient to Him as you learn to walk His way.

I was confident on that Saturday that Randy would not let me fall. I pray that you are confident today that God will not let you fall, regardless of how small your shuffling steps or how many times your hand falls off that bar called obedience.

I sense that it is time for many standers to stop being witnesses to the spiritual progress in other hurting men and women and for them to start learning and doing all that

God has for them. Marriages are restored by running the race, not reading the reports.

By the way, when movement started returning to my motionless leg, I was alone. A pre-dawn storm awakened me, and lying in my hospital bed, I started doing the exercises the therapists had taught me. I had to turn on the light to confirm what I thought I had just experienced. Sure enough, I could make the top bed sheet move by wiggling my great toe ever so slightly.

Most likely, as you progress in stander therapy, learning how to walk God's way toward a restored marriage, your progress will come when you are alone with Him. Please be careful not to confuse progress which often comes in the valleys, with plateaus which are often on the mountaintops. All you need to do is get in the habit of being alone with God, in the quiet places He will speak directly to you, in so many ways.

There's work to be done in your stander therapy that you must do. You cannot grow in the Lord by us doing it for you. May today you stop depending on what happened to someone else and start to exercise and learn all that God has especially for you. If you will be faithful in doing your spiritual exercises, you will be walking in love again soon.

"Even to your old age and gray hairs I am he, I am he who will sustain you. I have made you and I will carry you; I will sustain you and I will rescue you." **Isaiah 46:4**

IT IS HARD FOR A PRODIGAL WHEN. . .

- Nothing I say or do seems to shock or upset you.

- "I forgive you" is uttered as often as my name.

- "Don't worry about it" is your answer to everything I have done.

- You let me talk about you-know-who and you just listen and pray knowing that it is better for me to talk to you about the other person.

- I see you growing spiritually when I am living in sin.

- You build me up to our kids so they still love me.

- You have zipped your lips.

- You are content to live with almost nothing.

- You agree to anything and everything I ask.

- You depend on Jesus, not me, to be your Provider.

- I can't push your buttons like I once did.

- You make it impossible for me to hate you or even dislike you.

- You seem to remember all the things I like.

- You remind me that you will be waiting until you die.

- I know the home I left could always be my refuge from the storms of life.

- I suspect everyone is reminding you how I will never change, and how old dogs don't learn new tricks. I am not a dog and I am not out to learn tricks. I set out to be happy without you, but every time you show me unconditional love instead of anger and attempts to get even, something is being changed in my heart, one small bit at a time.

- People are also probably telling you not to be a doormat for me, but they have it all wrong. You are not being a doormat, but a welcome home mat.

The prodigal said: "I never loved you." The Lord said: ". . .I have loved you with an everlasting love;. . ." **Jeremiah 31:3**

The prodigal said: "I am never coming back." The Lord said: *He who goes out weeping, carrying seed to sow, will return with songs of joy, carrying sheaves with him. **Psalm 126:6***

The prodigal said: "Stop praying for me!" The Lord said: *"Bless those who curse you, pray for those who mistreat you." **Luke 6:28***

The prodigal said: "I hate you." The Lord said: *"Everyone who does evil hates the light, for fear that his deeds will be exposed." **John 3:20***

The prodigal said: "You act so holy." The Lord said: *For God did not call us to be impure, but to live a holy life. **1 Thessalonians 4:7***

The prodigal said: "You are a hypocrite." The Lord said: *"Do not judge, or you too will be judged." **Matthew 7:1***

The prodigal said: "I don't know what to do." The Lord said: *"Come, follow me," Jesus said, "and I will make you fishers of men." **Mark 1:17***

How do I know all those things wayward spouses say? Sadly, they have each been uttered in our home. Today, as you prepare to face another day without your spouse serving the Lord, look through the eyes of faith at the morning note your mate will leave you, in God's timing.

THE LONGEST MILE

The Mighty One, God, the LORD, speaks and summons the
earth from the rising of the sun to the place where it sets.
Psalm 50:1

Have you ever had God remind you of something years
after it happened? The forgotten event suddenly comes to
your mind when you are doing something totally unrelated.
That's what happened to me recently on a Sunday, as God
reminded me about the longest mile I have ever traveled.
The memories came rushing back while I was watching a
televised church service.

Do you suppose my longest mile is one of those traveled as
a 10-year-old kid with my parents aboard a Greyhound bus,
leaving grandparents in Kentucky to start a new life in
Florida? Certainly that was difficult, but our family was
filled with hope of a new life in Florida. So that could not
have been my longest mile.

How about that fall after high school when I traveled to
Cincinnati to attend mortuary science college? It was my
first time away from home, but I was filled with hope of
someday becoming a funeral director. So that was not my
longest mile.

Perhaps it was the one mile between my parent's home and
Charlyne's parent's home, on the way to pick up this new
girl for our first date? No, that could not have been the
longest, because I was so excited.

During the next 10 years there were three trips to the
hospital transporting a very pregnant wife. Those trips
seemed pretty long, as my wife moaned with labor pains.
Each trip was tempered with the hope of soon bringing
home a newborn son or daughter.

Do you suppose my longest mile was the afternoon when I loaded everything I owned into my car and moved to a low rent motel? No, Satan had filled my head full of sinful fantasies that I was about to act upon. Yes, certainly it was hard, very hard, to drive away from the only home we ever had, leaving behind a devastated wife and three children. The enemy had told me exactly what he has told hundreds of thousands of other prodigal spouses. He said that everyone was going to be all right, but I had to watch out for myself. After all, did I not deserve some happiness?

Years later, there were two trips to the cemetery to say goodbye on this side of eternity to my parents. Even those long miles were made bearable knowing that my parents had gone to life eternal with our Lord Jesus.

My longest mile was traveled on a Sunday afternoon in 1986, just before sunset. I was driving west on PGA Boulevard in Palm Beach County, preparing to angle onto Highway 710. No, there was no accident involved, nor was there car trouble. In fact, no one except my God and I had any idea what was transpiring inside my car.

I was alone, returning to my "pigpen" after visiting my children and parents in Pompano Beach. My destination was Okeechobee, 100 miles from home, still seeking that happiness through sin that Satan had promised.

As background to my longest mile, I was doing well by the world's standards, a funeral director at one of the two funeral homes in all of Okeechobee County. It was a place said to have 2,000 people and 4,000 cows. I was among a handful of men in that community who went to work every day wearing a suit and tie. So I attracted attention from females. I was living alone in a two-story townhouse.

To the world, it appeared that I had recovered from a divorce and was happily single. No one suspected that I was dying inside, filled with guilt and shame over having left my family. No matter how frequent the conquests, true happiness escaped me. Yes, I was in church every Sunday. Would you expect any less from a funeral director who was also on the prowl?

My longest mile came at that time of day when driving west into the setting sun is not bothersome, but sunset had not yet come. I had a passing thought, "What do I have waiting for me about 50 miles ahead in Cow Town?" I thought about my job, my apartment, and female friends. Somehow I realized that none of those things could ever fill the void in my life that was about 50 miles behind in my rearview mirror. I thought about my wife, my kids, my parents and our home. I just thought about my life, the chapter behind me and the chapter ahead of me, and they did not compare.

Driving on Highway 710 toward Indiantown with the late day sun beaming across those flat pastures and into my driver's side window, I now know that God was speaking to me, calling me to turn around and go home and not continue on to Okeechobee.

I did not know for the longest time that God had been reminding me of where I was going versus what was waiting at home. I passed it off as just being lonesome and continued on. Even the thoughts of my sinful plans for the week would not temper what I was feeling. I drove on, but with what I felt was almost a strong magnetic pull, trying to get my car to go back to Pompano.

The people were amazed when they saw the mute speaking, the crippled made well, the lame walking and the blind seeing. And they praised the God of Israel. **Matthew 15:31**

Yes, we do have our own free will as people want to remind you so often, but God has 10,000 ways to get our attention when our free will does not align with His will for our lives. He could have allowed me to crash into a pine tree that afternoon, or at least have the car engine blow up. Instead He allowed me to continue on as I was going. However, His calls to me became louder and louder.

You're probably wondering how soon after that Sunday afternoon I went home. It must have been at least a year later. In my attempt to get away from the pain, an indescribable pain that I was experiencing deep within, I moved from Okeechobee to Ft. Pierce. I could have moved 4,000 miles instead of only 40, but the conviction of God on my life would have always been one step ahead.

This week, every time I read an email or a letter with some sincere stander telling Charlyne or me how nothing seems to be happening in their prodigal's life, I am going to be reminded of my longest mile. Charlyne will learn about my mile when she reads this message. It has been over 23 years since God dealt with me on that Sunday afternoon.

Does God speak to prodigals? Yes, yes, a thousand times yes. Your beloved may not realize it is God, but someday they will. I pray that you will continue to pray and fast, and to stand, confident that your mighty God is dealing with your beloved this very day in response to your prayers. If you could see the spiritual war that is going on in the heavenlies, with your spouse's soul going to the victor for all eternity, we would not read how anyone's standing is "too hard." If you see all that is happening it would be easy to stand, because that would require no faith. God wants to see you depend on Him alone.

*What if some did not have faith? Will their lack of faith nullify God's faithfulness? Not at all! Let God be true, and every man a liar. . . **Romans 3:3-4a***

Please accept the word of one who has traveled that longest mile. God is at work in your prodigal spouse's heart and in their life every day, in response to your prayers. Since it

happened to me, as my wife prayed, I can say with the
hymn writer that, "It is no secret what God can do."

*Therefore, since we have been justified through faith, we
have peace with God through our Lord Jesus Christ,
through whom we have gained access by faith into this
grace in which we now stand. And we rejoice in the hope of
the glory of God.* **Romans 5:1-2**

AT GOLDEN POND

All of us also lived among them at one time, gratifying the cravings of our sinful nature and following its desires and thoughts. Like the rest, we were by nature objects of wrath. But because of his great love for us, God, who is rich in mercy, made us alive with Christ even when we were dead in transgressions—it is by grace you have been saved.
Ephesians 2:3-5

Each year July 4th is a countdown to celebrating one more year of a restored marriage on July 7. It still amazes me that I awoke that fateful 1987 morning with no intention of returning home. Six hours and a hundred miles later, I was again Charlyne's husband, forgiven by both God and by my wife.

Charlyne and I talk much about what brings prodigal spouses home, as well as what keeps them away. God has given me a burden to share from a prodigal's perspective, an issue that could be a roadblock to healthy marriages, as well as to prodigals coming home.

The subject is sensitive so I visited the *Charlyne Cares* page to see if my burden was even appropriate to mention. The first thing I saw was a banner proclaiming, **"Helping To Stop Divorce God's Way."** That was my license to discuss this delicate topic with you.

Let me share a very personal incident that happened long before I even started school. It took place one Saturday over 55 years ago, but I can still recall the details. I was tagging along with my dad and another male family member on a short road trip. We had stopped in Golden Pond, KY at a dairy that had an ice cream stand. After ordering, my dad and the other man were doing some nudging of each other and exchanging knowing smiles. At first, I did not know what they were reacting to. I stood on my tiptoes and peered over the ice cream counter and saw

232

that the female scooping ice cream was wearing a low-cut dress. Once back in the car, nothing was said. On that day, sitting in the back seat, eating an ice cream cone, young Bobby Steinkamp determined that men enjoyed sneaking peeks into low-cut blouses.

Modesty in dress is a topic that my wife and I discuss often. Charlyne and I have talked about how to tactfully address the subject, but until July 4, neither of us had the nerve. On July 4, while eating lunch, I turned on the television to watch the news. The anchorwoman was wearing a revealing dress, so I changed channels. On the second station, the weather lady was dressed in much the same way. Suddenly, memories of ice cream at Golden Pond came rushing to my mind. The Lord was telling me to take a stand for modesty.

I acknowledge that you and I may be from different generations. Styles may change, but decency and godliness do not. Certain parts of the body should not be exhibited in public in any generation, be it the first century or the twenty-first century; or should clothing be worn to accent those body parts, for the purpose of attracting attention from the opposite sex.

Whatever happens, conduct yourselves in a manner worthy of the gospel of Christ. **Philippians 1:27**

"So what does this have to do with marriage restoration?" Everything, my sister and my brother.

Brothers, you and I have a responsibility to our wives, to our marriages and to our God to treat every woman as a sister. That may mean changing the channel or looking the other direction when we could take an unholy glance in a store. It may mean not complimenting the inappropriate appearance of a co-worker, who has dressed to receive compliments and gazes.

Sir, I realize this is the style of modern fashion, but you and I both know how quickly our thoughts can take us from an "innocent" peek into adultery in our hearts. The ladies may not want to acknowledge what study after study has demonstrated about a man's zero-to-sixty-in-an-instant sexual thought process and how easily and often, it is ignited.

Here is the acid test for every man. Would we want another man looking at our wife in the way we are looking at another woman? Would we want any other man thinking those thoughts about our wife that we are thinking?

"I can't help what I think," someone is offering. Dwight L. Moody, the famed evangelist of another era compared our thoughts to a hotel. "You can't help who walks through the lobby," Moody said, "But you have all the control over who gets a rented room."

Sister, why do you dress that way? Do you know what men are thinking when they see those tight jeans or too short shorts? Are you aware of what is exposed when you lean forward?

You may feel I am out of line today, but I earned my now-discarded merit badge in lust the hard way. The price our family paid for it was a divorce. Thankfully I had a praying wife who would not give up until God brought me to my senses. While I was gone, if Charlyne had said she was standing but was dressing to attract glances (or stares) from other men, a huge obstacle would have been placed in my path home.

"Do you want me to dress like I am in a convent?" If that is what it takes for you to dress with modesty and decency, that is what I (and every honorable man) would appreciate you doing.

"High necklines are not fashionable today." Neither is standing for a prodigal spouse, and you are doing that. So decency in dress should not pose a problem for you.

"Bob sounds fired up." Yes, Bob is very fired up. God created sex to be between a husband and wife, but the enemy is using dress (or maybe lack of dress) in an attempt to get me and millions of other men to have inappropriate sexual thoughts. I sense that some of the women dressing immodestly are not even aware of what they are doing to the minds and hearts of men.

There are four words Charlyne and I hear far too often from our new people. **"They met at work."** I also have a merit badge from 25 years ago for pretending to be an attentive husband, listening to what my wife is saying, while my thoughts were on a female co-worker.

Let's look at two scenarios. Jack works in an office with several women. Some are very modern in their dress. Each day at work is an adventure to see how low the necklines plunge. Their hair is perfect and they smell so good. At quitting time, Jack goes home to his wife who is wearing jeans and a sweatshirt and has been chasing pre-schoolers all day. That night, is Jack thinking about an exhausted wife who talks too much, or the women who will be waiting at work the next day?

"You have heard that it was said, 'Do not commit adultery.' But I tell you that anyone who looks at a woman lustfully has already committed adultery with her in his heart." Matthew 5:27-28

Jill is one of those women in that office. She has a husband of her own, but after years of marriage, he has put on weight and seldom notices how she looks when leaving for work. Jill dresses (and acts) to catch the stares and comments of her co-worker, Jack. Before long, Jack and Jill fall down the hill. Senseless things happen and families are nearly destroyed. The beginning can be traced back to the provocative way someone dressed.

Charlyne and I have a female friend of many years. Years ago, she was in a similar situation to the fictional Jill. She found the Lord and He changed her. As long as we have known this woman, she has been modest in her dress. Beyond that, each time she bends forward in the presence of a man, she tactfully places a hand on her chest, as if pledging to the flag. In addition to covering anything that might be revealed, this woman is announcing "I'm not interested in your peeks." Charlyne and I pray that woman's husband might come to appreciate the gem of a wife he has praying and waiting.

Most of the standers we know are praying their spouse will be surrounded by godly influence. Would you want someone dressed like you, or peeking like you, to be an influence on your prodigal spouse? You might be the only godly example someone else's prodigal has. You and I cannot change all of society, but we have full control over our own lives, how we dress, what we do and how we represent Jesus.

Let us behave decently, as in the daytime, not in orgies and drunkenness, not in sexual immorality and debauchery, not in dissension and jealousy. Rather, clothe yourselves with the Lord Jesus Christ, and do not think about how to gratify the desires of the sinful nature. **Romans 13:13-14**

There is a tendency for some abandoned wives to look for affirmation from other men as a salve for their self-esteem. They dress to catch second glances. This is often done without regard for the potential harm to their already-fractured marriage.

Charm is deceptive, and beauty is fleeting; but a woman who fears the LORD is to be praised. **Proverbs 31:30**

The Golden Pond incident has never been shared publicly until today. I sense God has a reason for our revealing one more family secret. My prayer is that you will not take this counsel to be judgmental of either male or female standers. As with so much of what Charlyne and I do, when God shows any area to us that will help save marriages, we will proclaim that thought. My friend, let's be cautious how we attract looks (and where we look) so that marriages might be saved and restored, to the glory of God.

As a prisoner for the Lord, then, I urge you to live a life worthy of the calling you have received. **Ephesians 4:1**

WHAT WOULD BE DIFFERENT?

Am I now trying to win the approval of men, or of God? Or am I trying to please men? If I were still trying to please men, I would not be a servant of Christ. **Galatians 1:10**

There are a host of benefits to the one-flesh relationship that God creates between a husband and wife through marriage. There are even greater benefits of that relationship to a couple who are in ministry together. If you have been communicating with Rejoice Marriage Ministries for any length of time, the odds are that Charlyne and I can put our heads together and recall things about you and your marriage without benefit of the computer.

Nevertheless, we still have in our database the names of tens of thousands of families who have contacted us at one time or another. Beyond that, there are hundreds or even thousands of people who read *Charlyne Cares* each day who have never contacted us, and we know nothing about them.

With this number of people, from time to time we will receive an "I can't do this any longer" message. The good news is that this does not mean the end to an individual's stand with God for marriage restoration. Many of these people are having a tough day, and before long we receive a second message explaining how they are once again standing strong.

Most standers have, at one time or another, given thought to giving up. That seems to be an idea that Satan runs through the head of every person who has ever contemplated marriage restoration. Charlyne admits she had those days when we were divorced and she was standing.

May I ask you a question? If you totally forgot about standing for your marriage today, what would be different about tomorrow? Would your circumstances really change because you gave up hope? I trust that you would still pray, fast, read your Bible and have time with the Lord just as you are doing today.

The apostle Paul, writing in **Galatians Chapter 1**, almost seems to be writing to a discouraged stander, the person who heard from God about their marriage but is now contemplating, "getting on with life" and going a different direction:

I am astonished that you are so quickly deserting the one who called you by the grace of Christ and are turning to a different gospel — which is really no gospel at all. Evidently some people are throwing you into confusion and are trying to pervert the gospel of Christ. But even if we or an angel from heaven should preach a gospel other than the one we preached to you, let him be eternally condemned! As we have already said, so now I say again: If anybody is preaching to you a gospel other than what you accepted, let him be eternally condemned! **Galatians 1:6-9**

Sadly, all too often "getting on with life" could be translated "I have met someone and have allowed the enemy to take over my thoughts about a possible relationship with that person." Anyone who has heard or read very much from my wife knows in their heart of hearts about the covenant of marriage and that when you are married, a relationship with another person of the opposite sex will more often than not end in sin.

Apart from feeling free (*not being free*) to pursue or to be pursued by the opposite sex, not much would be different if you gave up your stand right now. Are you giving up your Christian faith? Are you giving up all hope that God can work miracles? If so, who will be there for you to call on when a bad diagnosis comes from the physician? If your finances are a disaster today, they will probably still be a disaster tomorrow, but you will not have God's provision to meet your needs.

If you are a stander with disobedient children, does giving up on your stand when things are tough mean that at some point you could also give up on your children when their disobedience becomes too much to handle? If you are caring for elderly parents are you going to give up on them when the going gets rough? How will you ever maintain and be successful at a job if you are quitting one of the most important assignments God has ever given you?

I am saying firmly that, if God has called you to stand and you make a decision not to stand, you are being disobedient to our Lord God Almighty. That is a serious matter.

Some might say, "I am not sure God ever called me to do this." Right there could be the problem. Before a crisis of belief hits, we each must lock in on our calling from God to do His will.

"The Spirit of the LORD will come upon you in power, and you will prophesy with them; and you will be changed into a different person. Once these signs are fulfilled, do whatever your hand finds to do, for God is with you." **I Samuel 10:6-7**

God calls specific people to specific assignments for specific purposes. Every person who has ever been called by God had a free will. Any of them could have thought, "What would be different?" and walked away from their assignment, often with disastrous results. What if Noah had quit, or if Daniel in the lion's den had said, "Why pray? What would be different?"

The Bible gives us examples of people who did say "What would be different?" and doubted God's power. Moses comes to mind, he did not see the Promised Land because of his unbelief. (Are you going to eventually see the promised land of your marriage or are you going to doubt God's power and fail?)

The Christian faith we enjoy today has been built upon thousands of years of God's people being obedient to His leading and refusing to ask, "What would be different?" but instead going ahead and following God by faith. Your family members and future generations are going to be living on the firm foundation of marriage restoration that you are building today.

Everything that would be different if you gave up on the assignment God has called you to would be negative. We also need to look at one more aspect of "What would be different?"

What would be different for your prodigal spouse if you give up your stand? Over 20 years ago my wife prayed me out of a sinful single lifestyle, keeping me out of Hell. Beyond that she prayed me through an illness 13 years ago when I was not expected to survive. Then she prayed me through a second illness two years later, so serious that I had a minister in my hospital room offering his larger church for a funeral service. She also prayed me through a serious cardiac crisis two years ago when the doctors did not know how I survived.

Our immediate family, now numbering 15, has been through more crises than can be listed, ranging from health to vocational to financial. Charlyne has been the primary prayer contact for each emergency. Our children, their spouses and now our grandchildren know that my wife is a person of prayer, who never turns away when a situation looks bleak.

How did Charlyne develop a reputation as a person of prayer? It did not come from sending out daily devotionals, nor by writing books. Neither did it come from her Bible study messages. It started with her stand for marriage restoration and continued as our kids and grandkids saw God answering her prayers.

I am alive today and serving God because I have a wife, which even though she asked "What would be different?" during her stand, weighed the alternatives and continued to stand strong, despite all the temptations and despite all the obstacles. For the sake of your prodigal, I am praying that you will continue to stand strong.

"What would be different?" Our Lord God is growing you as a Christian each and every day that you stand and pray and wait. Standing is simply discipleship in the Christian faith. Each day you wait for your marriage to be restored, you need to be growing a bit more like Jesus. People who are growing are excited and not about to walk away from what God has called them to do. May that describe you.

I press on toward the goal to win the prize for which God has called me heavenward in Christ Jesus. All of us who are mature should take such a view of things. And if on some point you think differently, that too God will make clear to you. Only let us live up to what we have already attained. **Philippians 3:14-16**

A VALENTINE'S GIFT GUIDE FOR PRODIGALS

(What's Hot and What's Not)

If I speak in the tongues of men and of angels, but have not love, I am only a resounding gong or a clanging cymbal. If I have the gift of prophecy and can fathom all mysteries and all knowledge, and if I have a faith that can move mountains, but have not love, I am nothing. If I give all I possess to the poor and surrender my body to the flames, but have not love, I gain nothing. Love is patient, love is kind. It does not envy, it does not boast, it is not proud. It is not rude, it is not self-seeking, it is not easily angered, it keeps no record of wrongs. Love does not delight in evil but rejoices with the truth. It always protects, always trusts, always hopes, always perseveres. Love never fails. . . And now these three remain: faith, hope and love. But the greatest of these is love. **I Corinthians 13:1-8,13**

As I reflected on what I could give to you for Valentine's Day, I thought about a question we hear often during early February: "Should I give my prodigal a Valentine's gift?" Only God can answer that question, because our answer may not be His plan for you. I can give some general suggestions on what's hot and what's not for prodigal spouses.

• Your Prodigal Could Use Your Prayers -

The prayers of a faithful, standing spouse, are the best gifts you can give to a wayward spouse. Don't be like the standers who write us, telling how they pray "all day every day" for their mate. Charlyne could not have done that, for she had to work and care for a home and three children by herself. I was confident that after the day ended and my wife was alone, her promises to pray for me were being fulfilled, regardless of how exhausted she might be. Jesus taught us to pray, so may you make time to pray for your spouse.

- **Your Prodigal Could Use Your Patience -**

"Was Charlyne always patient when you were divorced?" No, she was not, but once she had heard from God regarding the future of our marriage, that all changed. Much like you, your spouse is living in a turbulent, confused state right now. Showing your spouse patience would be a welcome gift by them.

- **Your Prodigal Could Use Your Permission -**

I have shared previously about the day that Charlyne told me, "I read something that may help you." The words she then shared about living with one foot in each of two worlds were timely in my decision to come home. She was saying, "I understand . . ." and not, "I demand . . ."

- **Your Prodigal Could Use Your Perseverance -**

From the first time I heard my wife utter the word "standing," over 24 years ago, right up until today, I have known one thing, my wife was not about to give up on what God had promised for her marriage. Along the way, I heard that she would still be waiting in her rocking chair when she was 80, and that I might miss the best part of our marriage. She was not giving up on me, because God was not giving up on me, even when I was living in sin. What an amazing demonstration of love, for me to know that I had an "ex" who was not about to walk away because of circumstances.

If you want a super gift to give to your prodigal for Valentine's Day, determine today that you will never, never, never give up on the one you love. If you give up and stop praying, who will be there to pray for their protection and for them to come to Christ?

I am grieved when good people, whom God has called to stand, give up because a friend told them to find someone else, or who say they will stand only until the non-covenant marriage is legalized, or until there is a child born into the other relationship. They may be standing today, giving up tomorrow, but standing again by the end of the week. If you want a great gift for your prodigal, lock down in your heart and mind, once and for all that you are standing until God does what He has promised you He will do, regardless of what happens tomorrow.

Just as there are "hot" gifts, there are also some "what's not" that you need to avoid handing to your spouse for Valentine's Day:

- **The Prodigal You Love Has No Use For Your Threats -**

Statements sounding like, "If you don't have that check here on time, I'm going to . . ." or, "I will tell my attorney to . . ." should never originate with a serious stander. Another great gift for your prodigal is to get the term, "I understand" back into your vocabulary.

- **The Prodigal You Love Has No Use For Your Condemning Tongue -**

Believe me, your prodigal spouse knows everything they are doing wrong, without your telling them. Each time you remind them, you are stacking more chips on the "reasons I can't go home" side of the table. The battle for your family will be won on your knees, in prayer and not with a sharp tongue slicing and dicing your mate.

- **The Prodigal You Love Has No Use For Your Temper -**

"Did Charlyne have a temper when you were divorced?" In the beginning, she had such a temper that I was afraid of what she might do. Her temper is another area where God touched my wife after she became serious about standing for our marriage. She has not been the same since.

- **The Prodigal You Love Has No Use For Your Taunts -**

Yes, you may win the battle if you disrupt their plans, but in the end, if you don't correct your ways, you will lose the war for your home. That other person is not your enemy, so even if you manage to manipulate until they are out of the picture, Satan will send someone else along.

- **The Prodigal You Love Has No Use For Your Trespasses -**

No matter how many times my wife teaches about not spying on a wayward spouse, people who call themselves standers continue to do so, often at the expense of their marriage. For the sake of your family, please stay out of your prodigal mate's personal property and activities.

I do not recall ever mentioning this before, but there were times during our divorce that I baited Charlyne to see if she would snoop. I remember one weekend leaving a note from the other woman inside our son's suitcase. I had folded the note in a particular way so that I could tell if it had been opened and read. The note was returned to me without having been opened. Charlyne passed every sordid test I sent her way, to the glory of God.

- **The Prodigal You Love Has No Use For Your Tough Love -**

How many times have you and I blown it in our Christian walk, yet each time our Heavenly Father forgives us and allows us to start over again? Jesus demonstrates unconditional love, not tough love, to His children. When standing for marriage restoration, we have an opportunity to be like Jesus by showing unconditional love to a spouse who has wronged us. Tough love is saying to a spouse, "If you don't do right, I will do wrong." That does not sound like words from Jesus.

Well, there's my list of what's hot and what's not for prodigals this Valentine's Day. Did God give you any ideas on what to get the one you love? I pray that He has.

This Christian walk called "standing" is so basic. It is no more than living and walking as Jesus would. It is responding to each of the enemy's tactics as Jesus would respond. Yes, standing is basic Christianity with feet, but at the same time it is the most difficult walk you may ever do as a Christian.

Do you know why it is so difficult for you to stand strong? The evil one hates families so much that he is throwing every conceivable obstacle at you, to convince you that your beloved will never change; that God has someone better for you; that He wants you to be "happy" and all the rest. (By the way, God's concern is that you be holy before you are happy).

This is the time of year when tourists we call "snowbirds" invade South Florida by the tens of thousands, escaping frigid northern winters. Along with the snowbirds, come the con artists, always attempting to make a fast dollar. One way they do this is by peddling knock-off merchandise at our local flea markets. Their counterfeit products may look much like the real item, but they are always constructed so cheaply they will not last for long, if they work at all.

Where are you going to get your prodigal's Valentine's gift? Granted, you can pick up Prayers, or Patience, or Permission that look (and sound) like the real deal at a low price, but once the test of the storms of life are applied, your gift will last about as long as a brand name purse purchased at a discount from the swap shop.

How, then, do you get gifts that last for your prodigal spouse? By your first having a close, personal walk with your Lord Jesus Christ. Your counterfeit gift may even be enough to draw your prodigal home, but it takes the real thing to have a mate home, happy, and ready to work on rebuilding a damaged marriage.

Regardless of when you read this, there is still time to get the perfect Valentine's gift for your prodigal spouse. You can obtain it on your knees. The price has already been paid at Calvary, by our Lord Jesus. Today, ask the Lord to give to you the Fruit of the Holy Spirit.

"But I never see my spouse. How will they even see the changes in me?" Trust me, the one you love will see (or hear) about the changes in you, once you totally sell out to Christ and to your marriage. It might be like the day, when I was picking up our children, that I asked Charlyne what had changed about her. She replied, "Nothing's different." I walked away from our door thinking it must be her hair that had changed. Months later, I would learn that it was her heart, not her hair that was different. I pray that your prodigal spouse may have reason in the days ahead to make that same discovery.

May you have a blessed Valentine's Day, even if you are alone today. Remember God loves you with an everlasting love, and He asks us each to share that love with others, even when they seem not to deserve love.

"A new command I give you: Love one another. As I have loved you, so you must love one another. By this all men will know that you are my disciples, if you love one another." John 13:34-35

THEY SAW AND BELIEVED

Early on the first day of the week, while it was still dark, Mary Magdalene went to the tomb and saw that the stone had been removed from the entrance. So she came running to Simon Peter and the other disciple, the one Jesus loved, and said, "They have taken the Lord out of the tomb, and we don't know where they have put him!" So Peter and the other disciple started for the tomb. Both were running, but the other disciple outran Peter and reached the tomb first. He bent over and looked in at the strips of linen lying there but did not go in. Then Simon Peter, who was behind him, arrived and went into the tomb. He saw the strips of linen lying there, as well as the burial cloth that had been around Jesus' head. The cloth was folded up by itself, separate from the linen. Finally the other disciple, who had reached the tomb first, also went inside. He saw and believed. John 20:1-8

Jesus is alive! All around the world, people are preparing to celebrate the resurrection of our Lord and Savior, Jesus Christ on Sunday. It is both sad and shocking that 50% of the married people in the United States will not wake up on Easter, the grandest day of the Christian year, with their spouse at their side. The enemy is wreaking havoc in our families, our churches, and in society, through divorce. Jesus is the answer.

If that describes you, Resurrection Sunday is your day. The disciples thought all hope was gone when Jesus was crucified. No doubt someone told those first Christians to "get on with life," just as people are telling you today. An empty tomb bore the testimony that the crucified Jesus was alive! His empty tomb bears testimony that your dead-appearing marriage is also alive. While you wait and pray for that day of restoration for your family, this Easter has some lessons for the stander.

- *We fret over rolling away the stone -*

When the Sabbath was over, Mary Magdalene, Mary the mother of James, and Salome bought spices so that they might go to anoint Jesus' body. Very early on the first day of the week, just after sunrise, they were on their way to the tomb and they asked each other, "Who will roll the stone away from the entrance of the tomb?" **Mark 16:1-3**

To the world, the huge boulder of adultery, addiction, or abuse appears to have been set in place in front of your marriage. The two Marys did not even need to question who would roll away the stone. God had that all worked out, just like He has for your stone.

- ***Some falter in their run to the tomb -***

When they came back from the tomb, they told all these things to the Eleven and to all the others. It was Mary Magdalene, Joanna, Mary the mother of James, and the others with them who told this to the apostles. But they did not believe the women, because their words seemed to them like nonsense. Peter, however, got up and ran to the tomb. Bending over, he saw the strips of linen lying by themselves, and he went away, wondering to himself what had happened. **Luke 24:9-12**

Who first saw evidence of the resurrection? The ones who went to see the tomb. The standers who first see evidence of marriage restoration are men and women who are "running" a straight line toward that goal. Your words may seem like nonsense to others, but you should only be listening and believing what the Lord speaks to your heart.

- ***Some forget the promise -***

While they were wondering about this, suddenly two men in clothes that gleamed like lightning stood beside them. In their fright the women bowed down with their faces to the ground, but the men said to them, "Why do you look for the living among the dead? He is not here; he has risen!

Remember how he told you, while he was still with you in Galilee: 'The Son of Man must be delivered into the hands of sinful men, be crucified and on the third day be raised again.'" Then they remembered his words. **Luke 24:4-8**

What has God promised you regarding your marriage? The Scripture tells us that God keeps His promises. Nevertheless, standers forget, even when God remembers. Time and time again, God reminds each of us not only what He has promised to do for us, but also of what He has called us to do.

- *Some forget it is Jesus -*

As she wept, she bent over to look into the tomb and saw two angels in white, seated where Jesus' body had been, one at the head and the other at the foot. They asked her, "Woman, why are you crying?" "They have taken my Lord away," she said, "and I don't know where they have put him." At this, she turned around and saw Jesus standing there, but she did not realize that it was Jesus. **John 20:11-14**

We acknowledge that the circumstances of your marriage make it look hopeless, but that is when Jesus works the best. Do not make the mistake of forgetting who brought the answer. May you realize that it is only Jesus. He is your hope for your hopeless circumstances.

- *Some fear Jesus is gone –*

Now Thomas (called Didymus), one of the Twelve, was not with the disciples when Jesus came. So the other disciples told him, "We have seen the Lord!" But he said to them, "Unless I see the nail marks in his hands and put my finger where the nails were, and put my hand into his side, I will not believe it." A week later his disciples were in the house again, and Thomas was with them. Though the doors were locked, Jesus came and stood among them and said,

251

"Peace be with you!" Then he said to Thomas, "Put your finger here; see my hands. Reach out your hand and put it into my side. Stop doubting and believe." Thomas said to him, "My Lord and my God!" Then Jesus told him, "Because you have seen me, you have believed; blessed are those who have not seen and yet have believed." **John 20:24-29**

We could wonder if doubting Thomas was the first stander? After the resurrection, Jesus entered the room without using a door, and instructed Thomas to place his fingers in the wounds on Jesus' hands. Thomas had said that would be the only way he would believe Jesus was alive.

What must Jesus do for you before you acknowledge that He is Lord and that He can restore your hurting marriage? Every day, and in every way, Jesus is showing us that He lives. Nevertheless, many times we follow Thomas' example of unbelief.

We pray that during Holy Week, you might seal your relationship with the risen Lord Jesus. He alone is the One who forgives, forgets, heals, and restores. May you call out to Him now.

Later Jesus appeared to the Eleven as they were eating; he rebuked them for their lack of faith and their stubborn refusal to believe those who had seen him after he had risen. He said to them, "Go into all the world and preach the good news to all creation. Whoever believes and is baptized will be saved, but whoever does not believe will be condemned." **Mark 16:14-16**

AN OPEN LETTER TO DADS

Sunday is Father's Day, but my heart is broken when I think about the children who have no father in their lives. For some of these, their father has died. For most, however, their father simply decided to quit being a dad. Before that happened, these men decided to quit being a husband. They listened to the voice inside that lied with statements like, "You deserve to be happy," or "You married the wrong person." That voice soon changed to, "Divorce isn't really so bad," and "The children will get over it."

How can I be so sure about those silent voices? In 1985 I walked out on my wife, Charlyne, and our three children. It was two years before I could discern between which relationship was real love and which was counterfeit. I had been blinded to the truth, just as you may be today.

Our children are being destroyed by divorcing parents. The greatest terrorist attack we need to fear is the terror of divorce. Society is allowing those horrible strikes on 50 percent of families and doing so little about it.

Charlyne and I get angry at hearing about teenagers who must be sent away because they are out of control. It makes us mad to hear of an elementary child, written off by a teacher because of behavior problems that started after parents divorced.

My prodigal friend, may I ask you a question? Why are you more concerned about your kicks than your kids? When did your anatomy become more important than your adolescent? Why are you cultivating sin instead of a son? When did a little thrill become more important that a little girl? Good times have replaced God's times. Booze has replaced the Bible. Pornography has replaced prayer. Our goal has become happiness, not holiness.

Don't worry, because the "experts" have told us that those we should love the most will get over the child abuse of divorce. NO! They will not! Precious children are being damaged for life by the selfish acts of parents, taken captive by the enemy, and listening to the world's advice.

I wish it were possible for the experts to leave their glass towers for a day and come help my wife and I answer our mail. What do we say to the parent who must sell their family home, the place of security for their kids, because the breadwinner is taking his bread somewhere sinful? How do we respond to a man whose thirteen-year-old daughter has become sexually promiscuous, just like her mother? What do we tell someone when the police, not the parents, have become involved in the discipline of a hurting kid? What can we do for the parent of a toddler who goes to sleep night after night sobbing the name of a missing mommy or daddy?

Do children "get over" that painful parental amputation that we call divorce? Not from where we sit. If you have walked out on your family, study after study, demonstrates that your kids will be handicapped for life, starting with poorer grades and ending with a shortened life span.

I left my wife and our three children for the very things I have written about here. There was evidence of damage being done in each of their lives that Charlyne and I do not share publically. I could not see beyond what "I" wanted.

There came a day when the Lord told me to go home. While I was gone (over two years), the Lord had been changing my wife. I went to her office and asked her to marry me all over again. Somehow, God worked out all the details. That was seventeen years ago.

This Father's Day weekend, we have three young adult children, their spouses, and seven grandchildren planning my Father's Day celebration. There is no thrill in the "far country" that can compare with having my young grandson console me, "Grandpa, Father's Day is for grandpas too!"

Books titled, "How To. . ." are the most popular with readers. For Father's Day, I want to give you, "How To Find Your Way Home." My book is subtitled, "Regardless of the Circumstances." Here it is: If you are serious about giving your family the best Father's Day gift possible, all contact with that other person must stop instantly. Period. End of sentence. That means no friendship, no "How are you doing?" phone calls, no driving by, no cards on birthdays. That other person does not "need" you. Your family needs you. When you move out, take someone else with you, or better yet, have them pick up your things.

That other relationship was not love, but lust. The only way to end lust is to starve it. If you continue contacts, you are only fertilizing your fantasies. You can never see or talk to that other person alone again. If you can do this for six months, starting on Father's Day, you can be preparing for Christmas with your children, without feelings for that person haunting you.

If you are sensing something in your spirit (I could not put Charlyne out of my mind), go for it and go home today! The first stop on the way needs to be on your knees, asking God to forgive you for what you have done. He will work out every obstacle that you are considering right now. Just wait until your kids hear that you are home!

Dad, you have a family waiting and praying for you who really needs you home. I will never forget July 7, 1987, when I suddenly remarried my wife. May this Father's Day be that kind of day for you.

Make this a Happy Father's Day for your family.

TESTING THE WATERS-SOMETHING TO PONDER

But Mary treasured up all these things and pondered them in her heart. The shepherds returned, glorifying and praising God for all the things they had heard and seen, which were just as they had been told. **Luke 2:19-20**

The story is told of the small church that called a new pastor. On his first Sunday morning he preached from John 3:16. That night, he preached a different sermon, but used John 3:16. The following Sunday he again preached on John 3:16. After church dismissed, the deacons thought they had a problem, so they met with their new pastor to ask why he was using John 3:16 every service.

"It's simple," the pastor explained. "Our people haven't grasped the meaning of John 3:16 yet."

You have heard it from my wife and me so many times that it might be like our "John 3:16," but here it is once again today: Your prodigal will make false starts on their journey home. During this holiday season the one you love may be testing the waters of your love, as well as the waters of life at home.

Charlyne and I cringe each time we hear or read something similar to, "We were getting divorced, but my spouse came home yesterday and our marriage is restored today." There is a process to marriage restoration. May I suggest you continue to read *Charlyne Cares*?

During the next six weeks, in response to the Holy Spirit moving on the lives of prodigals during the holidays, with memories of home, there will be lots of testing the waters. Men and women who walked out on their spouse and family will be coming around home and getting together with forsaken families. The prodigal's purpose in doing this is often to see if they are wanted back at home.

Many standers confuse any overture from their spouse as marriage restoration. Please remember that marriage restoration is a process that starts when a spouse returns home to live. Having a prodigal spouse drop in during the holidays is not in itself marriage restoration.

Prior to placing a child for adoption a home visit is made by the adoption agency. That in itself is not an adoption. It is someone checking out how things are at that home to determine if it would be a loving environment for nurturing a child. Prodigal spouses make the same type of visits back home, often staying more than one day. Then they leave again. This is where the road forks, with one route leading to permanent marriage restoration and the other leading to a painful detour on the way to restoration.

Let's look at our typical couple, Jack and Jill. During early December prodigal Jack shows up unannounced at the door of the family home where Jill lives. She is both shocked and thrilled to have him there, as are their children. For about 48 hours things appear as if nothing ever happened. On the third morning, without any explanation, Jack says he has to leave.

What happened? Jack was testing the waters at home. He may leave, but he is leaving with fresh memories of his family.

Jill has two options. The preferred way of handling a prodigal spouse testing the waters and then leaving is to do so with unconditional love. There would be no pressuring Jack for an explanation, nor would there be condemnation. Yes, Jill would be hurting deeply, having thought that Jack was home to stay. Somewhere along the way Jill would have been able to work, "I understand" or similar thoughts into conversation with Jack. Her husband would leave that home knowing that the door was open for his return at any time. Jill's hurts would be shared with the Lord and not with Jack.

Let's look at a detour road that Jill's actions could have sent her on. Instead of being like Mary, and pondering what was happening in her heart, as soon as Jack appeared Jill might have emailed all of her friends that her marriage was restored. On the morning that Satan pulled Jack out of the home once again instead of an "I understand" conversation, Jill would have demanded answers. There would have been a lot of accusations and possibly that statement uttered that Satan delights in hearing; "You have not changed."

Instead of Jack driving away from that home filled with guilt but assured that he would always be welcome there, Jack drives away angry, determined to never step foot in that house again.

Back inside, instead of Jill heading for her prayer closet, she is headed for the keyboard, ready to share with any who will listen how her husband came and went, that their restoration fell apart. That is not true. Jack came home to test the waters. The only one who did anything wrong was Satan, who pulled Jack back.

The first Thanksgiving we were apart, I asked if I might come to Thanksgiving dinner at our home. Charlyne refused. I ate a frozen turkey dinner alone in a hotel room. Once the Lord touched my wife to stand for our marriage, there was another Thanksgiving where Charlyne drove 100 miles into the far country to bring me dinner. Which Thanksgiving do you suppose contributed most to the restoration of our marriage?

My prayer is that this message will not come across as harsh. We are in a battle alongside you for the survival of your marriage. When our Commander has revealed to us where the enemy is lurking, it is our responsibility to share it with you, our fellow soldiers in this spiritual war.

For over 20 years, Charlyne and I have heard of the spouses returning home during this season. The pull of the holidays is more than they can resist. Prodigals return home first to test the waters, and then they return home to stay if they feel welcome.

When your prodigal spouse appears over these holidays, my wife and I pray that you will seek God's guidance in what to do. Please do not allow people to tell you, but listen to your Lord God who is never wrong.

Remember, restoration is a process that often starts with a prodigal spouse testing the waters. When the person you love comes by, in effect dipping a toe into the water, may you remember not to shove them in. It is equally important that you not banish them from the pool. Please allow God to do His mighty work in His time.

Charlyne has been calling the Rejoice family to special prayer during November and December for the restoration of marriages. When the one you love contacts you during the holidays, always remember it is an answer to prayer. God will bring restoration, but in His timing.

All mankind will fear; they will proclaim the works of God and ponder what he has done. Let the righteous rejoice in the LORD and take refuge in him; let all the upright in heart praise him! **Psalm 64:9-10**

CHRISTMAS "I" TROUBLE

When they saw the star, they were overjoyed. On coming to the house, they saw the child with his mother Mary, and they bowed down and worshiped him. Then they opened their treasures and presented him with gifts of gold and of incense and of myrrh. **Matthew 2:10-11**

Two weeks from today is Christmas Day. That does not seem possible. It must be either because Charlyne and I are getting older, or a sign of the times, but time seems to fly by. Actually, the old adage is true, time flies when you're having fun. Charlyne and I are having fun, ministering to friends around the world and witnessing marriages being healed and people coming to Christ.

About this time every year, people seem to develop "I" trouble. They lose their joy and their hope because their focus is on themselves, instead of on Jesus, whose birth we celebrate, and on the people around them. May I share some of the classic comments that are symptoms of "I" trouble?

- "They got a Christmas bonus and I didn't."

- "I don't hear from my spouse like other standers do."

- "How can I go to Christmas events when I have to go alone?"

- "I am not receiving many Christmas cards."

- "I am so defeated, down, and depressed."

- "I have financial problems."

- "I have no time."

- "Why should I even get a Christmas tree?"

- "Why should I read testimonies when I do not have one?"

- "Wonder what I will get for Christmas?"

- "I dread Christmas."

For most of us, including yours truly, there are both "amens" and "ouches" in that list. Let's look at what we might do to change some things.

It is as simple as getting rid of the "I" trouble. You do not need an ophthalmologist, but a Heart Doctor, our Lord Jesus, to correct your outlook on Christmas. If we can take the focus off ourselves, and put it on to Jesus, and others, I can promise you that your outlook will change.

May I ask you a question? What have you done for someone else this Christmas season? Not just a gift to someone's Christmas fund, but how much of yourself have you invested into making Christmas joyful for someone else?

If you reply, "You don't understand. I am going through a divorce," you, my friend, are not getting it. You can lose your hurts by becoming involved in helping others. Charlyne and I suspect that too many standers are spending Christmas on the computer. Instead of looking down at a keyboard, look around at the people you could be blessing by acts of love this Christmas season.

Speaking of looking around, last Christmas, tens of thousands of South Floridians looked up to see a sky writer aircraft carefully spell out, "God Loves You." It was soon followed by a second part, "Turn to Jesus." Someone had made a clever investment into the lives of many people.

While I have been sharing the cure for "I" trouble, a song about your eyes has been running through my mind:

"Turn Your Eyes Upon Jesus"

"O soul, are you weary and troubled? No light in the darkness you see? There's light for a look at the Savior, and life more abundant and free!

"His words shall not fail you-He promised, Believe Him and all will be well; Then go to a world that is dying, His Perfect salvation to tell!

"Turn your eyes upon Jesus, Look full in His wonderful face, And the things of earth will grow strangely dim, In the light of His glory and grace."

(Copyright 1933;1944 Singspiration Music. Used by permission CCLI #173562)

If you are seeking a Merry Christmas and it seems to be escaping you, turn your eyes off the crisis, the confusion, the challenges, the courts, and the computer. Turn your eyes upon Jesus and upon His hurting children who you are in a position to help.

My prayer today is that you will have a quick recovery from Christmas "I" trouble. Yes, it is possible for you to both be blessed and to be a blessing to others. The letters on God's eye chart are not **"I"** but **"HE"** and **"THEM."** Stop looking down and start looking around, and your Merry Christmas will be there. Soon you will be viewing Christmas with 20/20 spiritual vision.

After Jesus was born in Bethlehem in Judea,. . . "Where is the one who has been born king of the Jews? We saw his star in the east and have come to worship him." **Matthew 2:1-2**

WALKING ON EGGSHELLS

We have heard from many standers who will be with their spouses for part of the Christmas holidays and they may be "walking on eggshells." That is Charlyne's terminology for what they will be doing Christmas morning and all this weekend from Texas to Tasmania.

As you read these words scores of men and women who are praying for the healing and restoration of their marriage, will be rejoicing that they are with the one they love, even if for only one day. At the same time they will be walking on eggshells, sensing everything they say or do is being judged by their visiting spouse. Some standers might even feel they are being compared to another person.

The rest of us have a responsibility to pray in a mighty way for the families who are together only for the Christmas holidays. The enemy will be busy, bringing false meaning to what is being said in those homes. The evil one will attempt to bring up sore subjects. The evil one was busy yesterday, attempting to burn turkeys, make kids misbehave, causing the wrong people to call. And yes, Satan will attempt to "unzip the lips" of many standers, encouraging them to blast their prodigals.

It will be so tempting to respond to a visiting prodigal's "Why didn't you cook my favorite?" by reminding the one you love that you barely had money for what is on the table, because they walked out on the family. Pray these standers listen to the Lord before they speak.

Our God is greater than anything the enemy can muster up! He can walk each of those couples through their Christmas eggshells without even a crack, if one person in that home is listening to the Holy Spirit, and if the rest of us get serious about praying for our brothers and sisters today.

What was your reaction to the above paragraph? Someone is thinking, "I had no spouse with me for Christmas, probably none for New Year's, and you expect for me to pray for the ones who do? I hurt too much myself today to worry about them. Why doesn't God send my mate around this weekend?"

God's timing is not our timing. Could He be testing you, to see if you are ready for His miracle? It might be YOU requesting prayer for a visiting prodigal next Christmas (or this New Year's Eve!).

"Let's go to Bethlehem and see this thing that has happened, which the Lord has told us about.". . .The shepherds returned, glorifying and praising God for all the things they had heard and seen, which were just as they had been told. **Luke 2:15b, 20**

There is a message for standers in this part of the Christmas story.

So they hurried off and found Mary and Joseph, and the baby, who was lying in a manger. **Luke 2:16**

May you continue to seek the Christ of Christmas during this special holiday weekend.

Let me share my version of the song, *Away In A Manger:*

Away in a manger, no crib for a bed, The little Lord Jesus laid down his sweet head; The stars in the sky looked down where he lay, The little Lord Jesus asleep on the hay.

Be near them, Lord Jesus, we ask you today, close by all the standers, and love them we pray; Bless all the dear children in their tender care, And bring back Prodigals to live with them there.

MAKE IT OR BREAK IT

And we know that in all things God works for the good of those who love him, who have been called according to his purpose . . . What, then, shall we say in response to this? If God is for us, who can be against us? **Romans 8:28, 31**

You might have read about our multiple separations prior to our divorce. We had a rocky marriage, almost from the honeymoon. From all of those years of our human attempts at working on our marriage, no period turned out to be make it or break it like Christmas week just before our divorce.

This week there was a plane crash in Miami, killing all 20 people aboard that flight. Within hours of that tragedy, reporters were interviewing a woman who had taken that same flight over 50 times. On the day of the disaster she had missed her plane, due to late Christmas shopping. When a local television station first thrust a camera on her, her eyes were wide and she was speechless. Later she was able to share her story of how she was alive because of one incident that delayed her. I cannot imagine the turn her life will take, after being spared from the same fate that claimed the life of many of her friends and relatives.

On this day before Christmas Eve, I want to share from my heart with a prayer that you might see yourself in this message and avoid the Christmas flight that took down our marriage.

By Christmas, we had been separated for six months. We had both signed our property settlement agreement and were waiting for a January court date and what we both thought was to be our final divorce and the end of our problems.

Looking back now, almost 20 years later, Charlyne and I both see how either of us could have taken one simple action that would have resulted in calling off our divorce. Instead, because of our personal bitterness, hard-heartedness, and revenge, we clung to our boarding passes that would get us on board a divorce.

Do not repay anyone evil for evil. Be careful to do what is right in the eyes of everybody. If it is possible, as far as it depends on you, live at peace with everyone. . . Do not be overcome by evil, but overcome evil with good. **Romans 12:17-18, 21**

Charlyne and I have shared about these previously, but please allow me to highlight a few Christmas events:

- I had my wedding band melted down and gave it to Charlyne as a Christmas gift.

- She refused my request to be allowed to come home for Christmas dinner.

- I was looking for my wife's replacement. (I did not know it was Charlyne after God changed her.)

- We made our three children, ages 6 to 16, pawns in our game of selfishness.

- I had my first date with someone else on Christmas Eve.

- Christmas night Charlyne called and offered to deliver Christmas dinner to me, but just before she did, the other woman called. Charlyne's offer was refused.

By New Year's Eve, we were on board our flight to divorce. The rest of the Steinkamp story is one or two years of crashing and burning until Jesus came to our help.

Within minutes of that plane crash in Miami, lifeguards on wave runners and surfboards were scouring the area, looking for survivors. That is what my wife and I are attempting to do for your family. Unlike that scene in Miami, there is life and hope and signs of survival and recovery of a marriage all around you. We are not about to give up searching and helping the victims of separation and divorce, but how much better if we can help prevent you from even getting on board the doomed flight of divorce.

This message will be read by both prodigals and standers alike. For that we are grateful, and we have a suggestion, regardless of which group you are in.

If soldiers fighting on both sides of the front lines of World War II can put down their weapons in observance of Christmas, why can't you? Every Christmas, we hear of prodigals who stop by home out of obligation. They like what they discover there, and simply stay, or start making plans for their return. Many, many, will continue to test the waters to be certain what they are witnessing is for real.

We hear of standers, who are led by the Holy Spirit to make some overture of kindness toward their prodigal, and that spark of unconditional love ignites something deep inside a hardened heart.

My friend, here it is two days before Christmas. For scores of marriages, it is make it or break it time. If God leads you to demonstrate love and forgiveness toward someone, do not hesitate out of fear of rejection. Your giving the invitation or showing kindness still hits home with your prodigal, even if your kindness is refused.

Therefore, as God's chosen people, holy and dearly loved, clothe yourselves with compassion, kindness, humility, gentleness and patience. Bear with each other and forgive whatever grievances you may have against one another. Forgive as the Lord forgave you. And over all these virtues put on love, which binds them all together in perfect unity. ***Colossians 3:12-14***

There are two options. (A) You can put down the weapons for Christmas, or (B) you can stand your ground, demanding what is yours, hanging on to the bitterness, anger, and revenge, making your spouse toe the legal mark for Christmas. Now do you suppose (A) or (B) will bring you closer to restoration?

Your doomed divorce flight is boarding, but if you will linger over Christmas, with the right heart, always looking to the Lord for His help and guidance, you just might miss that flight.

Christmas is a make it or break it time for so many individuals. What about you?

BE CONSISTENT

Against all hope, Abraham in hope believed and so became the father of many nations, just as it had been said to him, "So shall your offspring be." . . .Yet he did not waver through unbelief regarding the promise of God, but was strengthened in his faith and gave glory to God, being fully persuaded that God had power to do what he had promised. **Romans 4:18, 20-21**

We are only two days away from another new year, putting our divorce   one more year behind us. I realized that we now have six grandchildren older than our youngest son's age when we divorced.

On one hand, it seems like ages ago that we went through all of the horrible mess. I think about some of the things I did, while pretending to be a Christian and cannot believe that it was me. On the other hand, it seems like only yesterday that I suddenly walked back into the home where we still live today, but as a remarried husband.

On one hand, not much has changed. The church where we were remarried in the Pastor's office, still sits within walking distance, across the park from our home. Our children married and moved out, giving Charlyne and me each an office at home. Today they all have families of their own, but when the grandkids have "sleep overs," they stay in the former bedroom of their mom or dad. On the other hand, a lot has changed. My parents have both graduated to glory and no longer live down the street. Our home is where adult children confide in their parents, and where grandchildren stop by when they need batteries or a dollar.

I cannot look at the arrival of another new year without wondering how much different my life and Charlyne's life would be today, if she had followed everyone's advice and had given up on me. Yes, I could have convinced another woman that she needed me for a husband, but before long she would have also become a victim of my sin. I doubt that any woman on earth would have prayed for me during multiple life-threatening illnesses the way Charlyne did. No other woman would have forgiven my mistakes since remarriage the way my Charlyne has.

When I look back to the 1980's, I also have to wonder what Charlyne's life might have been like if she had started having coffee with a man from church, justifying, "We're just friends." You and I both know where the slippery slope of "just friends" usually leads, as we start enjoying the company of someone other than our spouse, and then start confiding in them, and then. . .

Each of the physicians Charlyne worked for had the "perfect man" for my wife. She was then in her late 30's, working in an administrative position, with a great personality, and divorced.

It was true that Charlyne deserved "someone better" than what I had been for the 19 years before we divorced. (In case you do not know, I was abusive, unfaithful, and guilty of quite a few more sins.) Anyone who heard our story would have told Charlyne, "God doesn't want you to live like that," and many people did.

The friends, pastors, doctors, and counselors were correct. Charlyne deserved someone better. God did not want her to continue living as she had been. God in His infinite wisdom, and according to His Word, did not give my wife a different husband. He gave her a new husband, in the same overweight, balding body of the man she had married in 1966, and who had fathered her children. Why did God do that? In answer to the prayers of a faithful but forsaken wife, who had taken a stand with Him and chosen to swim against the tide of popular opinion, against educated counsel and against the circumstances. My wife wanted to see our marriage problems fixed God's way.

If I could describe my wife in a word, what would I say? Friend? Wife? Lover? Teacher? Wise? Trustworthy? Honest? Godly? She is all those things, but above all else, my wife is consistent. From the day she got up from the church altar, on a Sunday in March, over two decades ago until this day, my wife has not backed down from what God told her to do, namely, to take a stand with Him, trusting Jesus to heal our home in His way and in His timing.

Of all my wife's good traits, the one that did the most to draw me home was her consistency. I attempted to push her buttons, but soon discovered time and again that they were disconnected. No matter what I said, no matter what I did, Charlyne stood firm that God was going to restore our marriage and rebuild our family. No matter what I needed, my wife was willing to give all she had.

The dictionary defines consistent as: "Marked by harmony, regularity, or steady continuity; free from variation or contradiction." That describes the woman I married twice.

Charlyne does not appreciate me making her a super stander, but that is what she was back then, and that is what she is today. From that eventful Sunday in March until I came home, not once did I hear my wife threaten to give up her praying and standing for me. I did hear about her waiting in a rocking chair until she was 80, and about how I was going to miss the best years of our marriage, but even those comments were always delivered with a smile.

I wonder how our lives might have been different if Charlyne had been inconsistent. What if I had heard over and over, "I was standing, but gave up. Now I am really standing for you." I knew in my heart that even if I had gone through a series of non-covenant marriages and fathered a child on every block, that consistent Charlyne would be standing with her Lord, praying and waiting for me.

During your marriage struggles, God has not called you to win a popularity contest among family, friends, pastors and counselors. He has called you to stand with Him for the salvation of your spouse and for their homecoming, both to the Lord and to their spouse.

Charlyne was consistent with her pastor. My wife had registered for an out–of–state faith conference. Her pastor called her in to caution her about getting "mixed up with that crowd." What did consistent Charlyne do? She loaded up her old car and attended that conference, where she was greatly blessed. Now that is swimming against the tide.

Charlyne was consistent with the other person. There was no hair-pulling, no name calling, no threats, when God allowed consistent Charlyne to sit in a restaurant booth across from the other woman and explain what God had called her to do. My wife expressed to the other woman that even if she and I married, Charlyne would be sitting in that rocking chair, waiting for me. That, my friend, is consistency.

Create in me a pure heart, O God, and renew a steadfast spirit within me. **Psalm 51:10**

Do you know what would be an answer to our prayers? For you to become a consistent stander, a person sold out to Jesus Christ, following His leading, doing things His way, being consistent in standing with Him for marriage restoration. If you could become consistent, day after day, week after week, month after month, and yes, even year after year, your prodigal spouse will sit up and take notice. The day will come when, like me, your beloved will sense in their heart of hearts, "Can't beat 'em, might as well join 'em." That is the point when prodigals come home.

A question I asked Charlyne more than once is a question that your absent spouse might also be asking, "What will be different if I come back?" Charlyne had an answer, just as you do. My wife demonstrated what would be different by her consistent living.

May I offer a word of warning? Consistent standing, like consistent Christian living, is observed and not announced. If you manipulate for your prodigal to get wind of your new consistent standing and then fail to do so, it will blow up on you faster than a defective New Year's Eve firecracker. Consistent standing is walking the walk, day after day, regardless of the circumstances, not simply talking the talk.

Every day people contact us. They buy books, tapes and CD's. Some of those people even openly state they are looking for Charlyne's "secret" to our restored marriage. Today I have given you the secret in a word: Consistency. There is no limit to what our Lord God could do if you seriously became a consistent Christian and a consistent stander. Above all else, people you love could be won to Christ Jesus by your example. For certain there would be changes in your life and in your Christian walk. Beyond that, no prodigal can stay away from the God personified by a consistent spouse, living as such, even in the midst of adversity. The prodigal for whom you pray will start to take notice, without you doing or saying a thing, after your life becomes consistent. Are you ready to start?

And the God of all grace, who called you to his eternal glory in Christ, after you have suffered a little while, will himself restore you and make you strong, firm and steadfast. **I Peter 5:10**

MEET THE STEINKAMPS

Bob and Charlyne's marriage was not always blissful. They separated several times and finally divorced in 1986 after 20 years of marriage and with three children.

Charlyne searched the scriptures and discovered that God hates divorce. She found that our Lord Jesus Christ restores and rebuilds marriages when a mate will love the prodigal unconditionally, as Christ loves us. Charlyne committed herself to a sacrificial stand for the restoration of their marriage. To the glory of God, Bob and Charlyne were remarried on July 7, 1987.

God allowed Bob and Charlyne to minister His love, forgiveness and restoration to others with broken marriages for over twenty years. In December 2010, Bob lost his battle with cancer and end stage heart disease. Today, Charlyne and her family continue to proclaim the message that *God Heals Hurting Families.*

You may be reading this book searching for someone to help your marriage problems and His name is Jesus. Please contact us if Rejoice Marriage Ministries can help you discover the difference that the Lord can make in your hurting or dead marriage.

But blessed is the man who trusts in the Lord, whose confidence is in Him. **Jeremiah 17:7**

THE GREATEST NEWS

*That if you confess with your mouth, "Jesus is Lord," and believe in your heart that God raised him from the dead, you will be saved. **Romans 10:9***

Many people in a hurting marriage have discovered that the first step in a healed marriage is to have a personal relationship with Jesus Christ. Our God and Creator is waiting to hear your prayer. Have you received Jesus Christ as Lord and Savior of your life? He will save you and be your Comforter and Counselor in the days ahead, regardless of the circumstances.

A Prayer For You

"Dear Jesus, I believe that You died for me and that You rose again on the third day. I confess to You that I am a sinner and that I need Your love and forgiveness. Come into my life, forgive me for my sins, and give me eternal life. I confess to You now that You are my Lord and Savior. Thank You for my salvation. Lord, show me Your will and Your way for my marriage. Mold me and make me to be the spouse I need to be for my spouse. Thank You for rebuilding my marriage. *Amen.*"

Signed_____

Date_____

*"...Believe in the Lord Jesus, and you will be saved -- you and your household." **Acts 16:31***

TEN SOURCES OF HELP

Here are ten ways that Rejoice Marriage Ministries, Inc. can help you stay encouraged as you stand strong with God and pray for the restoration of your family.

Prayer – The number one source of help for your marriage is centered on prayer. While we have several prayer lists and an online Chapel, our goal is to teach you how to pray for your prodigal, for yourself and for your loved ones.

The Bible – We strive to teach you how to get your answers from the Word of God. "Someone said," really should not carry much weight with what you do. Instead, read God's Word daily, seeking His will for your life and marriage. God does speak to His children.

Website – The Rejoice Marriage Ministries Website has over a thousand pages of helps, including Q & A, praise reports from standers, testimonies from restored marriages, audio teleconference recordings and much more to help you be able to stand for healing of your marriage. http://RejoiceMinistries.org

Charlyne Cares – Seven days a week we send subscribers a daily devotional by that name. Always based on Scripture, Charlyne teaches on topics that will help you grow in the Lord as you pray for your marriage. We also offer a men's devotional that is sent weekly. Subscribe for free from http://charlyne.org/

Stop Divorce Radio – We broadcast good music and Good News around the clock for men and women facing marriage problems. You will hear Charlyne and men of God teaching on marriage restoration. You can listen while you work or play. http://StopDivorceRadio.org

God Heals Hurting Marriages – Our five-minute weekday audio program. We encourage you to get into the habit of listening every day. You will be amazed how often the program's subject will be exactly what you need to hear for that day to be encouraged in the Lord.
http://rejoiceministries.org/radio.html

Fight For Your Marriage – A weekly 30-minute audio Bible study online. Charlyne teaches you God's Word on how to grow in the Lord, pray for your family and fight for the healing and restoration of your marriage.
http://rejoiceministries.org/radio.html

Stop Divorce Bookstore – Our online bookstore offers marriage restoration teaching in books and on CDs. We also have other items available, such as front license plates, bracelets and Spanish material. http://StopDivorce.org

Rejoice Pompano – Standers in South Florida meet with us here in Pompano Beach each month for Bible study, worship, prayer, support and fellowship. From time to time we also take Rejoice on the Road to other communities.
http://RejoicePompano.org

Personal Contact – Our goal is for you to develop a personal relationship with Jesus Christ. When He is Savior and Lord of your life, you can allow Him to direct every step in your life and marriage.

We have many other helps available for the man or woman who is seeking marriage restoration God's way. We encourage you to take advantage of the other resources available by visiting our website.

For nothing is impossible with God. **Luke 1:37**

Rejoice Marriage Ministries, Inc.
Post Office Box 10548
Pompano Beach, FL 33061

MY THOUGHTS ON STANDING

'Then the nations around you that remain will know that I the LORD have rebuilt what was destroyed and have replanted what was desolate. I the LORD have spoken and I will do it.' **Ezekiel 36:36**

MY THOUGHTS ON STANDING

'Then the nations around you that remain will know that I the LORD have rebuilt what was destroyed and have replanted what was desolate. I the LORD have spoken and I will do it.' **Ezekiel 36:36**

MY THOUGHTS ON STANDING

'Then the nations around you that remain will know that I the LORD have rebuilt what was destroyed and have replanted what was desolate. I the LORD have spoken and I will do it.' **Ezekiel 36:36**

MY THOUGHTS ON STANDING

'Then the nations around you that remain will know that I the LORD have rebuilt what was destroyed and have replanted what was desolate. I the LORD have spoken and I will do it.' **Ezekiel 36:36**

MY THOUGHTS ON STANDING

'Then the nations around you that remain will know that I the LORD have rebuilt what was destroyed and have replanted what was desolate. I the LORD have spoken and I will do it.' **Ezekiel 36:36**